# Access GCSE ENGLISH LANGUAGE for OCR

teachit.co.uk
ENGLISH TEACHING ONLINE

CW01621438

**Alison Smith**

Chris Barcock
Chief Examiner

Liz Hanton
Mel Peeling
Alison Ross
Christine Shaw Smith

OCR RECOGNISING ACHIEVEMENT
OXFORD UNIVERSITY PRESS
Official Publisher Partnership

# Contents

## Unit 3: Information and Ideas

# How to Use This Book

## Welcome to your GCSE English Language Course!

The aim of this book is to prepare you for your OCR GCSE English Language exam and Controlled Assessments. In the following chapters you will find plenty of fun and interesting activities to build your skills and knowledge, and all the help you need for your assessments.

This book includes a range of **useful features**.

- **How to approach** sections explain what you need to do for each part of your GCSE.
- **Preparing for** sections offer helpful guidance on preparing for exams and Controlled Assessments to help you achieve your best results.
- **Learning checklists** at the start of each chapter help to explain the Assessment Objectives and tell you what skills will be covered in the pages that follow.
- **Functional Skills** boxes allow you to use your GCSE knowledge in real-life tasks, helping you to prepare for the standalone Functional Skills assessments.

This book is made up of three units:

- **Unit 1:** Extended Literary Text and Imaginative Writing
- **Unit 2:** Speaking, Listening and Spoken Language
- **Unit 3:** Information and Ideas

Each of these units is assessed using **Assessment Objectives**. The four Assessment Objectives (AOs) for English Language are shown on the next page.

### AO1 Speaking and listening

- Speak to communicate clearly and purposefully; structure and sustain talk, adapting it to different situations and audiences; use Standard English and a variety of techniques as appropriate.
- Listen and respond to speakers' ideas and perspectives, and how they construct and express meanings.
- Interact with others, shaping meanings through suggestions, comments and questions, and drawing ideas together.
- Create and sustain different roles.

### AO2 Study of spoken language

- Understand variations in spoken language, explaining why language changes in relation to contexts.
- Evaluate the impact of spoken language choices in your own and others' use.

### AO3 Studying written language

- Read and understand texts, selecting material appropriate to purpose, collating from different sources and making comparisons and cross-references as appropriate.
- Develop and sustain interpretations of writers' ideas and perspectives.
- Explain and evaluate how writers use linguistic, grammatical, structural and presentational features to achieve effects and engage and influence the reader.

### AO4 Writing

- Write to communicate clearly, effectively and imaginatively, using and adapting forms and selecting vocabulary appropriate to task and purpose in ways that engage the reader.
- Organize information and ideas into structured and sequenced sentences, paragraphs and whole texts, using a variety of linguistic and structural features to support cohesion and overall coherence.
- Use a range of sentence structures for clarity, purpose and effect, with accurate punctuation and spelling.

# Unit 1

## Extended Literary Text and Imaginative Writing

UNIT 1

## HOW TO APPROACH UNIT 1

### How will this unit be tested?

This unit is worth 30% of your final mark. It will be tested by Controlled Assessment.

For this assessment you will complete two tasks:

- **Section A:** a response of up to 1600 words on an extended literary text.
- **Section B:** two pieces of imaginative writing with a total of up to 1200 words.

You will have **four** hours for each task but this might be split into shorter sessions. Before you write your responses in the Controlled Assessment, you will spend time preparing your work in lessons.

### What will the tasks be?

For **Section A** you will answer **one** question on **one** literary text. The text might be a novel, a play, poetry or literary non-fiction.

In **Section B** you have a choice of tasks. Whichever task you choose in Section B, you will need to produce **two pieces of writing**.

The task will **either** focus on:

- producing personal and imaginative writing, **or**
- writing prose fiction.

## SECTION A: EXTENDED LITERARY TEXT

### How will my work be marked?

Your writing in this section will be marked against Assessment Objective 3, which tests the skills listed below.

- Read and understand texts, selecting material appropriate to purpose, gathering evidence from different sources and making suitable comparisons and cross-references.
- Develop and sustain interpretations of writers' ideas and points of view.
- Explain and explore how writers use language, structure and presentational features to engage and influence the reader.

### When will the tasks be set?

The tasks are set a year in advance of the assessment, so there is time for you to study the text and your task in class before you write your final response.

# 1.1 Literary Texts: How Meaning is Constructed

**LEARNING CHECKLIST**

AO3

In this chapter you will learn to:

1. Understand texts, choosing parts that relate to certain ideas and comparing them where necessary.
2. Understand writers' ideas and points of view (viewpoints).
3. Explain how writers use language, style and form to interest the reader and to make the reader think a certain way.

## Meaning, ideas and influence

This chapter will help you improve your skills in reading and understanding poetry and prose. Once you understand the overall meaning of the text, you will practise making more specific points and supporting these points with quotations.

As well as identifying the main ideas, you will focus on how writers make a reader think in a certain way or feel a range of emotions.



**ACTIVITY 1**

What emotions might a writer try to trigger in a reader? Add words to a spider diagram or illustrate it with simple facial expressions.

## Understanding surface meaning

Before you can look in detail at a text, you need to understand what it is about. This 'surface meaning' is also known as the **literal meaning**.

# 'About His Person'
## by Simon Armitage

Five pounds fifty in change, exactly,
a library card on its date of expiry.

A postcard, stamped,
unwritten, but franked,

marked by the sorting office to show that it has been posted

a pocket-size diary slashed with a pencil
from March twenty-fourth to the first of April.

A brace of keys for a mortise lock,
an analogue watch, self-winding, stopped.

a pair

a secure lock set into a door

a watch with a clock face and two hands (rather than digital)

A final demand
in his own hand,

a rolled-up note of explanation
planted there like a spray carnation

but beheaded, in his fist.
A shopping list.

A giveaway photograph stashed in his wallet,
a keepsake banked in the heart of a locket.

No gold or silver,
but crowning one finger

a ring of white unweathered skin.
That was everything.

## ACTIVITY 2

**a** Look at the title of the poem on the left. What does it suggest the poem will be about?

**b** List ten things that are found on the man.

**c** Complete this sentence in your own words:
On the surface, 'About His Person' is about...
Choose a quotation from the poem to prove your point.

## Understanding implied meaning

Looking below the surface meaning to find the **implied meaning** beneath is called 'reading with insight'. This is an important skill that examiners will be looking for. Often the writer won't make the implied meaning obvious so you have to work it out.

In the poem 'About His Person' (see Page 9), there are lots of clues about the man's life and how he died. We have to look beneath the surface of the poem to work them out.

### ACTIVITY 3

Complete the grid below. What clues can you find about:

- the man's life?
- how he died?

| Clues from the poem | What this suggests about the man's life | What this suggests about how he died |
|---|---|---|
| 'a library card on its date of expiry.' | He liked to read books but maybe he couldn't afford to buy them. | It was about to run out so maybe he didn't see the point in renewing it. Maybe he knew he was going to die. |
| 'a postcard, stamped,/ unwritten, but franked' | Someone sent a postcard with no written message. Maybe the message was in the picture. This suggests a secret in his life. | |
| 'a pocket-size diary slashed with a pencil/from March twenty-fourth to the first of April' | | |
| 'a ring of white unweathered skin' | | |

UNIT 1

There are different ways of reading and understanding each clue. Your job is to be like a detective and make the best judgement you can based on the evidence you can find. To do this you need to look very closely at the words in the poem.

You then need to consider what effects these words have upon the reader. Writers often make readers think hard to decide what their words really mean. Words or lines that have more than one meaning can be described as **ambiguous**.

## ACTIVITY 4

**a** The poet tells us that the man had 'A giveaway photograph stashed in his wallet'. The word 'giveaway' is ambiguous. It could mean something free, or it could reveal something else about the man. What do you think it means? Explain your ideas to a partner.

**b** The phrase 'in his own hand' is also ambiguous. It could mean holding something, but what else could it mean? Could it mean two things? Explain why.

## ACTIVITY 5

The last line of the poem is: 'That was everything.' The surface meaning is that the poem has listed every item that the man had with him. What else could this line mean?

## Analysing language choices

In the novel *Tsotsi*, Athol Fugard describes life in a poor township in South Africa, where some young black people turn to crime and violence in order to survive. Tsotsi is a young black gang leader.

### ACTIVITY 6

In the extract below, Tsotsi sets out with his gang to commit a murder. Choose three examples where the writer makes:

- the township seem scary
- Tsotsi and his gang seem scary.

### From *Tsotsi* by Athol Fugard

The street they took was crooked and buckled as bad as the corrugated iron fences they passed on the side and Tsotsi led them a way that was sharp with stones, and eyes, and dog's teeth. It was dusty and the end of a day, but still light, when they left the room [...] the four men passing that moment were harbingers of the night, that moment gone now because *they* had passed and rooms were suddenly grey and cold and mothers calling their children off the streets where shadows were running like rats after the four pipers.

And Tsotsi knew it. Knowing it not only as a fact as big as the brave men who stepped aside to let him pass, and the shopkeeper who hurried out to board up his windows and bolt his door, or as small as fatherless children and the whispers of hate that scuttled away down the alleys, he knew it also as his meaning. Life had taught him no other. [...] The big men, the brave ones, stood down because of him, the fear was of him, the hate was for him. It was all there because of him. He knew he *was*. He knew he was there, at that moment, leading the others to take one on the trains.

That is why in his passing down the crooked street, men looked the other way and women wept into the dust.

buckled: crumpled

harbingers: people who signal the approach of something

pipers: refers to the old tale of the Pied Piper who cleared a town of rats by playing a tune to lure them away

Here is an extract from a student's response:

**STUDENT**

The writer makes the township seem scary when he says that the street is 'crooked' and 'buckled' which sounds really bad. It also sounds scary because of the dog's teeth and eyes, which sound like evil things are hiding in the dark. It is described as 'grey and cold' which also makes it seem like a bad place to be.

Look at how this student has put **short quotations** into the middle of her sentences. This is a good way to write because it shows the examiner that you can choose the most relevant words to prove your point. This student also explains what effect these words have on the reader.

### ACTIVITY 7

How does the language in the extract on Page 12 build up a sense of suspense about what is going to happen next?

To answer a question like this you need to:

- find examples from the text
- think about what they mean
- decide what effect they have on the reader.

Copy and complete the table below to help you to plan an answer.

| Quotations | What it means | Effect on the reader |
|---|---|---|
| 'mothers calling their children off the streets' | Mothers want their children off the streets because it is dangerous out there. | This makes the reader feel nervous because the mothers are trying to protect their children from something. |
| 'men looked the other way' | | |
| 'women wept into the dust' | | |

## The effects of language patterns

In *Of Mice and Men*, John Steinbeck uses language for different effects, for example to create realistic sounding speech or to show how tough life was in 1930s America.

Here, you will look at how Steinbeck uses images and **patterns of language** to create a setting in your mind and to bring his characters to life.

### From *Of Mice and Men* by John Steinbeck

[…] On the sandy bank under the trees the leaves lie deep and so crisp that a lizard makes a great skittering if he runs among them. Rabbits come out of the brush to sit on the sand in the evening, and the damp flats are covered with the night tracks of 'coons, and with the spread pads of dogs from the ranches, and with the split-wedge tracks of deer that come to drink in the dark. […]

Evening of a hot day started the little wind to moving among the leaves. The shade climbed up the hills toward the top. On the sand banks the rabbits sat as quietly as little gray, sculptured stones. And then from the direction of the state highway came the sound of footsteps on crisp sycamore leaves. The rabbits hurried noiselessly for cover. A stilted heron labored up into the air and pounded down river.

skittering: a light sound of quick running
brush: small trees and shrubs
'coons: racoons
stilted: long thin legs like stilts
labored: struggled
pounded: beat the air strongly with its wings

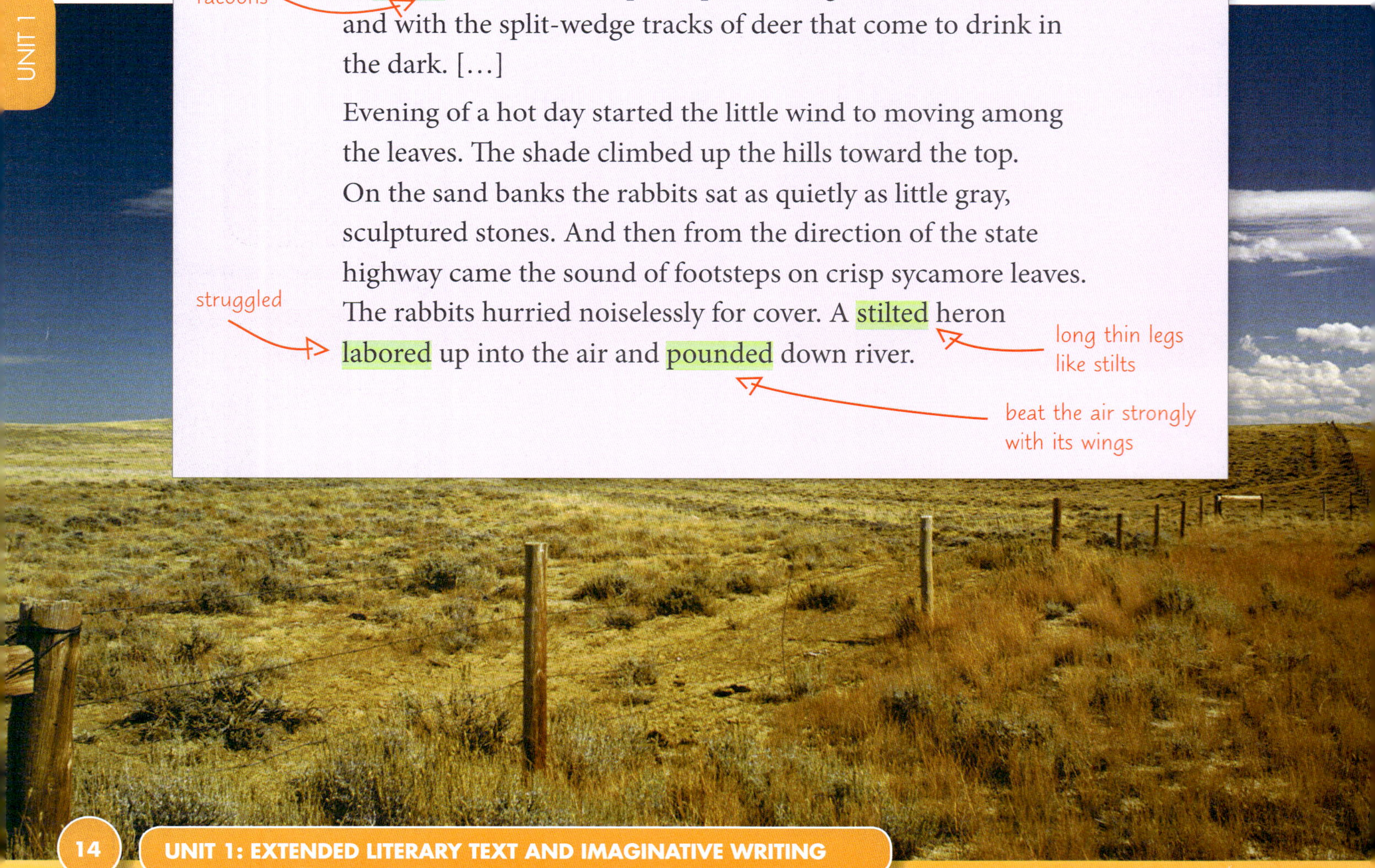

## ACTIVITY 8

**a** Read the description of the clearing on Page 14 and then complete the grid on the right, adding more rows.

**b** Which of the animals listed are described as making a sound in the extract?

**c** What other sounds are described in the extract?

| Animals mentioned in the extract | Do the animals appear later in the novel? If so, how? |
| --- | --- |
| dogs | Candy's dog is shot by Carlson. |
| | |
| | |

Animal imagery is a language pattern that Steinbeck uses in this novel. He uses it to help create convincing characters. For example, throughout the novel Lennie is compared to a number of animals.

## ACTIVITY 9

This spider diagram shows the animals that Lennie is compared to. Copy the diagram.

**a** Find quotations from the text where Lennie is described as or compared to the animals in the diagram. (Examples can be found in Chapter 1.)

**b** For each example, write down what this tells the reader about:

- what Lennie looks like
- what kind of a person Lennie is.

This example has been done for you:
Lennie is described as having a 'big paw'. This suggests that he is a big man. It might also mean that he is like a dog which always does what his master, George, says.

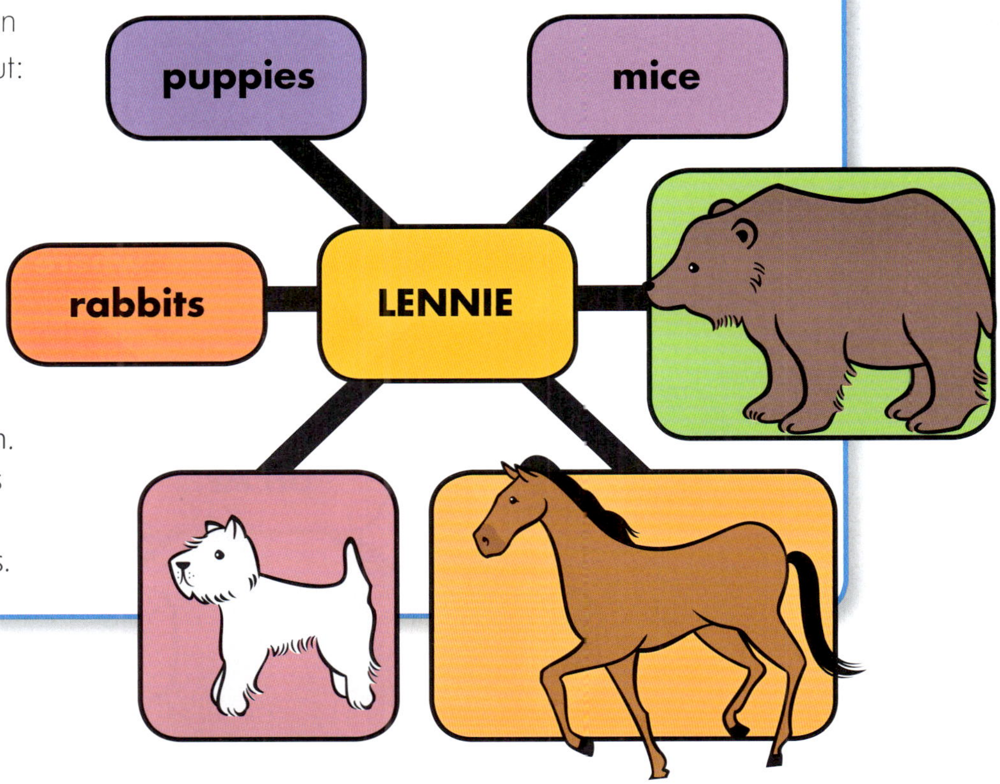

# 1.2 Evaluating How Texts are Interpreted

**LEARNING CHECKLIST**

AO3

In this chapter, you will learn to:

1. Understand texts, choosing parts that relate to certain ideas and comparing them where necessary.
2. Understand writers' ideas and points of view (viewpoints).
3. Explain how writers use language, style and form to interest the reader and to make the reader think a certain way.

## Responding to texts differently

Look at the image on the right. Do you see a beautiful young woman or an unattractive old woman? People see things in different ways. It's the same with words on the page – people can read them in different ways.

UNIT 1

### ACTIVITY 1

Which parts of your life and background might influence how you read a text? Copy and complete the spider diagram below, adding things that might affect the way your respond to what you read.

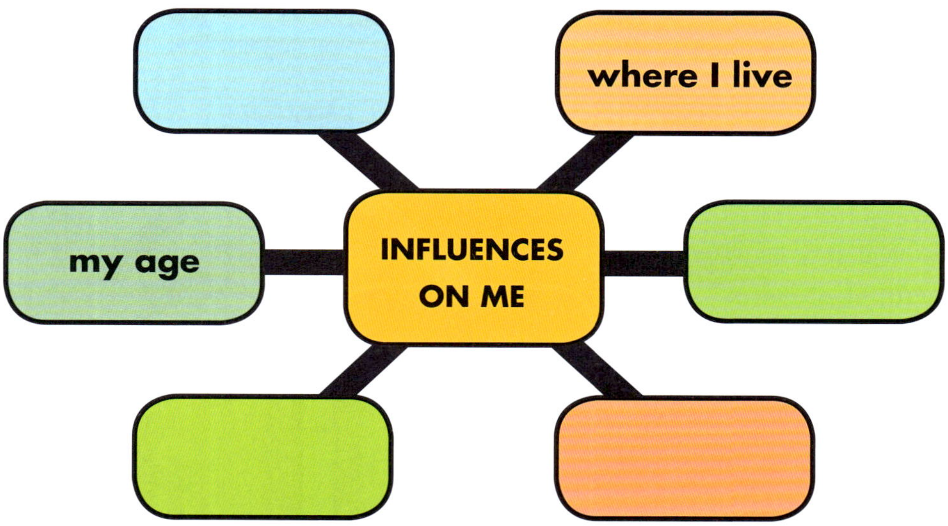

So, anything from **where** you come from to **when** you were born can affect what you read and how you interpret it.

## ACTIVITY 2

Read the view about men from the opening line of *Pride and Prejudice*: 'It is a truth universally acknowledged that a single man in possession of a good fortune must be in want of a wife.'

**a** What does 'universally acknowledged' mean?

**b** Is the statement true or false? Why?

**c** Look back at your spider diagram. Do you think this statement was true when the novel was written? Why?

## ACTIVITY 3

Read the extract from *Pride and Prejudice*, right, where Elizabeth tries to turn down Mr Collins's proposal of marriage.

**a** Why does Mr Collins think Elizabeth has turned him down?

**b** Why is Elizabeth surprised that Mr Collins is going to ask her again?

**c** A reader at the time might think this is funny because women were not meant to behave this way. Why might a modern reader find it funny?

### From *Pride and Prejudice*

**by Jane Austen**

'When I do myself the honour of speaking to you next on this subject, I shall hope to receive a more favourable answer than that you have now given me; though I am far from accusing you of cruelty at present, because I know it to be the established custom of your sex to reject a man on the first application, and perhaps you have even now said as much to encourage my suit as would be consistent with the true delicacy of the female character.'

'Really, Mr Collins,' cried Elizabeth, with some warmth, 'you puzzle me exceedingly. If what I have hitherto said can appear to you in the form of encouragement, I know not how to express my refusal in such a way as may convince you of its being one.'

more favourable answer – an answer that I like more
established – the normal way of behaving
application – proposal of marriage
to encourage my suit – to encourage me to try harder to get you to agree
consistent with the true delicacy – as fits the natural shyness
exceedingly – a great deal
have hitherto said – have said before

## Same place, different viewpoints

Some writers use their writing to show people what they think about something. That doesn't mean that the reader has to agree with them, though.

Morecambe is a seaside resort in the north west of England. Here is what Bill Bryson says about Morecambe in his travel book *Notes From a Small Island*.

### From *Notes From a Small Island*
**by Bill Bryson**

It is hard to say when or why Morecambe's decline started. It remained popular well into the 1950s – as late as 1956 it had 1,300 hotels and guesthouses, ten times the number it has today – but its descent from greatness had begun long before. The famous Central Pier was extensively damaged by a fire in the 1930s, then gradually sank into an embarrassing wreck. By 1990 the town officials had removed it from the local map – simply pretended that the derelict heap projecting into the sea, dominating the front, wasn't there. [...]

derelict heap: run down pile

Today Morecambe's tattered front consists largely of little-used bingo halls and amusement arcades, everything-for-£1 shops, and the kind of cut-price boutiques where the clothes are so cheap and undesirable that they can be safely put outside on racks and left unattended. Many of the shops are empty, and most of the rest look temporary. [...] So low had Morecambe's fortunes sunk that the previous summer the town couldn't even find someone to take on the deckchair concession. When a seaside resort can't find anyone willing to set up deckchairs, you know that business is bad.

deckchair concession: the place where you can rent deckchairs to use on the beach

And yet Morecambe has its charms. Its seafront promenade is handsome and well maintained and its vast bay (174 square miles, if you're taking notes) is easily one of the most beautiful in the world, with unforgettable views across to the green and blue Lakeland hills.

promenade: the walkway along the seafront

## ACTIVITY 4

Thinking of a writer's purpose can help you to decide whether to accept or question their opinions.

**a** Bryson may have had more than one purpose when writing his description of Morecambe. Choose at least two purposes from the list below:

- to persuade
- to describe
- to explain
- to entertain.

**b** For each purpose you have chosen, find a quotation from the extract to back it up. For example:

| Purpose | Example |
|---|---|
| To inform | 'as late as 1956 it had 1,300 hotels and guesthouses' |

# morecambe

Home | Visit us | More

Morecambe, with its spectacular bay, its wide-open skies and whirling seabirds, is preparing for a new tomorrow. Culture is at the heart of it and the pace is gathering. New shops, restaurants and coffee bars are quickly replacing the jaded arcades; art has been interwoven at every step and its crowning glory, The Midland, has been lovingly restored and updated.

## ACTIVITY 5

Read the description above, which appeared on the website for Morecambe Tourist Board.

**a** What is the **purpose** of this paragraph?

**b** Pick out **words** or **phrases** which show that this is a positive review of the resort.

**c** Why is there a difference in these two descriptions of the same place? **Clue:** think about the purpose of the texts.

**d** Who might agree with the tourist board's version and who might agree with Bill Bryson's version?

## Poetry of protest

At the start of the First World War, in 1914, posters such as the one shown below were common. They were produced by the government and displayed in public places, with the purpose of encouraging young men to join the army.

### ACTIVITY 6

Look at the poster on the right.

**a** What is the main message of this poster?

**b** Who is its audience? How can you tell?

**c** How do the **words** and **images** on the poster persuade men to join up?

Wilfred Owen was a poet and soldier. He was killed in action one week before the First World War ended in November 1918. Wilfred Owen wrote the poem 'Dulce et Decorum Est' in 1917.

## From 'Dulce et Decorum Est'
### by Wilfred Owen

Bent double, like old beggars under sacks,
Knock-kneed, coughing like hags, we cursed through sludge,
Till on the haunting flares we turned our backs
And towards our distant rest began to trudge.
Men marched asleep. Many had lost their boots
But limped on, blood-shod. All went lame; all blind;
Drunk with fatigue; deaf even to the hoots
Of tired, outstripped Five-Nines that dropped behind.

mud (sludge)

flares fired into the sky to light up the battlefield (haunting flares)

their feet all bloody (blood-shod)

exhaustion (fatigue)

gas bombs (Five-Nines)

### ACTIVITY 7

**a** What view of war does Owen present in this poem? Is it positive or negative?

**b** Give an **example** from the poem to prove your point.

**c** Compare the view in the poem with the ideas presented in the poster on Page 20. How is the message in the poem different from the poster?

## Considering alternative interpretations

Thomas Hardy's 'Tony Kytes, The Arch-Deceiver' was first published in the 1890s. It tells the story of Tony Kytes, who can't make up his mind which of three women to marry: Milly, Unity or Hannah, even though he is already engaged to Milly.

### ACTIVITY 8

From a modern point of view, the women in this story could be seen as figures of fun. Match each view of women in the left column to the quotation that appears to support it on the right.

| View of women | Quotation |
|---|---|
| **1.** Women's worth was based purely on their physical beauty. | **a.** 'Throw over Milly? – all to marry me! How delightful!' broke out Hannah, quite loud, clapping her hands. |
| **2.** Women were prepared to betray each other to win a husband. | **b.** 'My daughter is not willing sir!' says Mr Jolliver [Hannah's father], hot and strong. |
| **3.** Women had to do as their fathers told them. | **c.** 'If you like, Tony. You didn't really mean what you said to them?' |
| **4.** Women were weak, with Milly agreeing to marry Tony even though he has just proposed to two other women in front of her. | **d.** 'And – can you say I'm not pretty, Tony? Now look at me!' |

However, this is just one interpretation. It is also possible to say that maybe Hardy is:

- being critical of the **treatment** of women, rather than the women **themselves**
- or, using exaggerated female characteristics to make the behaviour of men, such as Tony, seem even more ridiculous.

Read the extract below from 'Tony Kytes, The Arch-Deceiver'. Tony is explaining to his father the mess that he has got into.

## From 'Tony Kytes, The Arch-Deceiver' by Thomas Hardy

'I only asked her – that is, she asked me, to ride home.'

'She? Why, now, if it had been Milly, 'twould have been quite proper; but you and Hannah Jolliver going about by yourselves –'

'Milly's there too, father.'

'Milly? Where?'

'Under the corn-sacks! Yes, the truth is, father, I've got rather into a nunny-watch, I'm afeard! Unity Sallet is there too – yes, at the other end, under the tarpaulin. All three are in that wagon, and what to do with 'em I know no more than the dead! The best plan is, as I'm thinking, to speak out loud and plain to one of 'em before the rest, and that will settle it; not but what 'twill cause 'em to kick up a bit of a miff, for certain. Now, which would you marry, father, if you was in my place?'

a mess

a large canvas sheet

get angry

### ACTIVITY 9

**a** How might this extract suggest that Hardy is mocking (laughing at) Tony, rather than the three women? Look carefully at what Tony says, how he says it and what this shows about him.

**b** Look at the student response to this question below. Complete the bits that have been missed out using quotations to back up each point.

**STUDENT**

In 'Tony Kytes, The Arch-Deceiver', the three women could be seen as the main figures of fun in the story. They are shown as shallow, vain and willing to betray each other to win a proposal from Tony. One of them even says...

On the other hand, Tony himself could be the main figure of fun in the story. He is shown as foolish and indecisive. He even has to ask his father's advice about...

# 1.3 Exploring Language Variation

**LEARNING CHECKLIST**

AO3

1. Understand texts, choosing parts that relate to certain ideas and comparing them where necessary.
2. Understand writers' ideas and points of view (viewpoints).
3. Explain how writers use language, style and form to interest the reader and to make the reader think a certain way.

## Language choice and audience

It is important that writers choose language that is suitable for their **audience** (reader). It is like choosing the right outfit for the right occasion.

### ACTIVITY 1

**a** Match each of the texts (A–C) below to the correct target audience (1–3).

**b** Explain your choices to a partner.

**c** Which is the most formal text and which is the least formal?

**A** Once upon a time there was a pink bunny called Bouncy Bob-Tail.

**B** Wot u up 2 later? party at mine 2nite c u there!

**C** Dear Madam, I am writing to you to express my concern about the amount of litter on our streets. The problem is becoming unbearable.

1

2

3

UNIT 1

## Language choice and purpose

A writer's choice of language will be linked to his or her **purpose**. Read the extract below from *Notes from a Small Island* by Bill Bryson. In the extract he describes his visit to the Stonehenge Gallery in the Salisbury Museum.

### From *Notes From a Small Island* by Bill Bryson

I was particularly interested in the Stonehenge Gallery because I was going there on the morrow, so I read all the instructive labels attentively. I know this goes without saying, but it really was the most incredible accomplishment. It took 500 men just to pull each sarsen, plus 100 more to dash around positioning the rollers. Just think about it for a minute. Can you imagine trying to talk 600 people into helping you drag a 50-ton stone 18 miles across the countryside, muscle it into an upright position and then saying, 'Right, lads! Another twenty like that, plus some lintels and maybe a couple of dozen nice bluestones from Wales, and we can party!' Whoever was the person behind Stonehenge was one dickens of a motivator, I'll tell you that.

Annotations: on the morrow – the next day; instructive – very informative; accomplishment – achievement; sarsen – large stone; lintels – the stone that goes across the top; bluestones – a type of stone

### ACTIVITY 2

**a** Use a copy of the grid below to decide what each quotation shows about Bryson's purpose. Tick the right columns to show the purpose of each quotation. Some quotations may have more than one purpose.

**b** In the final column, explain the effects of the language used in each quotation.

| Quotation | To inform | To entertain | To persuade | Effects |
|---|---|---|---|---|
| **1.** 'It took 500 men just to pull each sarsen' | | | | Use of facts to create an authoritative tone. |
| **2.** 'Right lads! Another twenty like that… and we can party!' | | | | |
| **3.** 'Just think about it for a minute.' | | | | |

## Benjamin Zephaniah: language choice

Lots of Benjamin Zephaniah's poetry is about injustice. Read the opening of his poem, 'Chant of a Homesick Nigga'.

### From 'Chant of a Homesick Nigga'
**by Benjamin Zephaniah**

There's too much time in dis dark night,
No **civilians** to hear me wail,
Just ghosts and rats
And there's no light
In dis **infernal** bloody jail.
I want my Mom
I want my twin
Or any friend that I can kiss,
I know the truth that I live in,
Still I don't want to die like dis.

If I had sword and I had shield
I would defend myself no doubt,
But I am weak
I need a meal or **barrister** to help me out,
I know my rights
Now tape dis talk
Of course I am **downhearted**,
Look sucker I can hardly walk
And the interview ain't even started.

You call me nigga, scum and wog
But I won't call you master,
The Home Secretary is not my God,
I trod earth one dread Rasta,
But in dis dumb, unfeeling cell
No decent folk can hear me cry
No God fearers or **infidel**
Can save me from dis **Lex Loci**.

civilians: people not in the armed forces

infernal: hellish

barrister: a lawyer who speaks for people in court

downhearted: miserable

infidel: a person who has no religious faith

Lex Loci: the law of a place

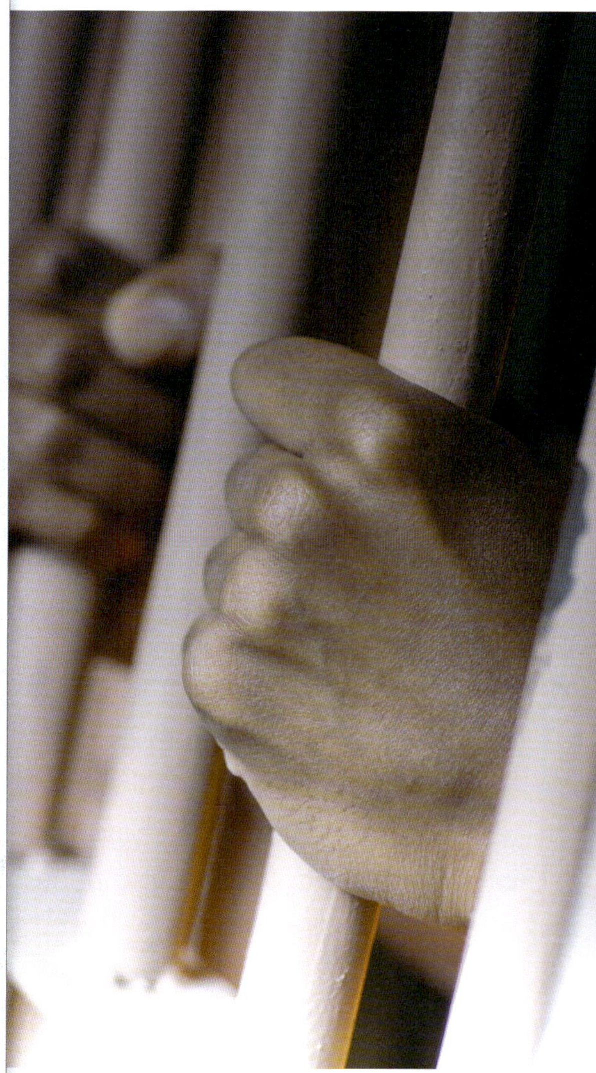

UNIT 1

## ACTIVITY 3

**a** Where is the narrator of this poem?
**b** Who is he speaking to?
**c** The poet uses the word 'dis' which is a dialect word meaning 'this'. Why do you think he uses a dialect word?
**d** Look at the use of offensive, racist language in this poem. Why do you think the poet chooses to use these words?

## ACTIVITY 4

The poem is a protest against injustice. Explain to a partner how Zephaniah uses the poem to do this. Use the bullet points below to help you.

- Look at how the narrator says he is treated.
- Look at what he says he would do if he could.
- Look at the language he uses.

## The M25 Three

The title of Zephaniah's poem 'Three Black Males' refers to Raphael Rowe, Michael Davis and Randolph Johnson. Called the 'M25 Three' by the newspapers, they were imprisoned in 1990 for murder and robbery. They claimed to be innocent and some of the victims stated in court that at least one of the robbers was white. In 2000 their convictions were overturned and the men were released.

UNIT 1

### 'Three Black Males'
### by Benjamin Zephaniah

Three black males get arrested
When they said they seek two whites,
Dis poet said that's expected
For we have no human rights,
We die in their police stations
We do nothing to get caught
We are only in white nations
When we win them gold in sports.

Three black males in the system
So the system just rolls on.
Can you recognise the victims
When the truth is dead and gone,
Can you recognise their **anguish**
When they beg you time to care
Or do you forget your language
When three black males disappear?

Raphael Rowe is not an angel
And Michael Davis ain't
Let us be straight and factual
Randolph Johnson is no saint,
The **Home Office** has a God complex
But that office is not great
For it does not recognise **subtext**
Injustice or mistakes.

Let all poets now bear witness
Let the storyteller tell
Let us deal with dis white business
Dis **democracy's** not well,
The cops, the judge and jury
Need some helping it does seem
And three black males with a story
Fight
So truth can **reign supreme**.

anguish: pain and suffering

Home Office: government department that deals with law and order

subtext: the meaning behind the words

democracy: a government where everyone gets an equal say

reign supreme: rule above everything

**The Daily News**

MONDAY JULY 17 2000 www.the-daily-news.co.uk

DAILY NEWSPAPER OF THE YEAR 50p

NEW Money Issues Section inside

# M25 THREE FREED BY APPEAL COURT

Freedom granted for innocent London trio after legal revoke

THE M25 THREE were dramatically freed yesterday at the Old Bailey. It occured that a leaked police report from 1999 found typed notes from Patrick Baker's police interviews, which had been heavily edited.

## ACTIVITY 5

**a** List five examples of injustice in the poem. Find a short quotation for each.

**b** Who is the poet talking about when he says 'we' in the poem?

**c** Who does he mean when he says 'you'?

## ACTIVITY 6

**a** The poet uses the word 'dis' several times in the poem. Why do you think he does this?

**b** Why do you think he repeats the word 'Let' at the start of the first three lines in the final stanza?

**c** How else does Zephaniah express his anger at the treatment of the 'Three Black Males'? Use the bullet points to help you.

- Think about repetition.
- Think about the words he uses.
- Think about the tone or mood of the poem.
- Think about the effect of the single word 'Fight' on a line by itself.

## Consolidating your reading skills

Read the question in Activity 7, then read the poem carefully. Write a response to the question, using the tips and advice on the next page to help you.

### ACTIVITY 7

What do you learn about the criminal in the poem? Explain your answer using evidence from the text. Think about:

- what the thief says
- what the thief does.

# 'Stealing'

## by Carol-Ann Duffy

The most unusual thing I ever stole? A snowman.
Midnight. He looked magnificent; a tall, white mute
beneath the winter moon. I wanted him, a mate
with a mind as cold as the slice of ice
within my own brain. I started with the head.

Better off dead than giving in, not taking
what you want. He weighed a ton; his **torso**,
frozen stiff, hugged to my chest, a fierce chill
piercing my gut. Part of the thrill was knowing
that children would cry in the morning. Life's tough.

*torso*: the main part of a body without any arms or legs

Sometimes I steal things I don't need. I joy-ride cars
to nowhere, break into houses just to have a look.
I'm a mucky ghost, leave a mess, maybe pinch a camera.
I watch my gloved hand twisting the doorknob.
A stranger's bedroom. Mirrors. I sigh like this – *Aah*.

It took some time. **Reassembled** in the yard,
he didn't look the same. I took a run
and booted him. Again. Again. My breath ripped out
in rags. It seems daft now. Then I was standing
alone among lumps of snow, sick of the world.

*Reassembled*: put back together

Boredom. Mostly I'm so bored I could eat myself.
One time, I stole a guitar and thought I might
learn to play. I nicked a **bust of Shakespeare** once,
**flogged** it, but the snowman was the strangest.
You don't understand a word I'm saying, do you?

*bust of Shakespeare*: a model of the head and shoulders of Shakespeare

*flogged*: sold

**The facts and advice on this page may help you to develop your ideas as you write a response to the question in Activity 7.**

Read the poem through several times.

The poem was inspired by a real-life event.

The poem was published in the 1980s, when 3 million people were unemployed.

What do you think about the structure of the poem? **Clue:** Why might the poem start and end with a question?

Use short quotations from the text to support your points.

Use phrases to show that more than one idea is possible, such as 'this might suggest' or 'this could show that'.

Look for patterns of language that might help you understand the more hidden meanings. **Clue:** In this case, look for words which suggest violence.

Is the narrator a totally evil character? Is there any reason to feel sorry for him or her?

# PREPARING FOR UNIT 1

## SECTION A: EXTENDED LITERARY TEXT

### What do I need to learn before the assessment?

By the end of your preparation you should be able to talk about the characters, themes and setting. You should also be able to discuss how the writer has used language and form to express his or her ideas. You will also need to know what might have influenced the writer and what his or her viewpoints are.

### Can I take notes into the assessment?

Yes. When you have finished your study of the text, you will have time to make some clear, well-organized notes. Your notes should be no more than **one A4 sheet** in length.

### What are controlled conditions?

Controlled conditions mean:

- You cannot talk to anyone.
- You are allowed to take in an **unmarked copy** of your text and your sheet of notes, but nothing else.
- If you are completing your response on computer, you cannot use a spell checker or have Internet access.
- You have to do all of the work by yourself.
- If the assessment is divided up into separate sessions, your work will be taken away from you at the end of each session and locked away by your teacher. You will not be allowed to have it back until the beginning of the next session.

# HOW TO APPROACH UNIT 1

## SECTION B: IMAGINATIVE WRITING

### What will the tasks be?

You will have a choice of either:

**Personal and imaginative writing:** something based on an experience you have had or seen

**or**

**Prose fiction:** something that may be based on an experience, but where you use your imagination to develop it into a new story.

The task will be split into **two** parts. Everyone does part '**a**', then for part '**b**' you will choose one of three tasks. Together, both parts are worth **30 marks**.

### How should I respond to the tasks?

Your part 'a' response should follow a sequence of events. Make sure that you describe the scene and characters clearly so that they seem real in the reader's mind. It is also important that your writing is accurate in terms of spelling, punctuation and grammar. Make sure you keep some time aside at the end of your assessment to check your work before you hand it in.

### How will the tasks be marked?

You will be marked according to Assessment Objective 4, which covers the skills listed below.

- Write clearly, with imagination, using a suitable form and words to engage the reader.
- Write with a clear structure and sequence in sentences and paragraphs, using a variety of language features and techniques.
- Use a variety of sentence structures to create different effects, with correct punctuation and spelling.

# 1.4 Personal and Imaginative Writing

AO4

## LEARNING CHECKLIST

In this chapter you will learn to:

1. Write clearly, with imagination, using a suitable form and words to interest the reader.
2. Write in sentences and paragraphs, using a clear structure and order, and a variety of language features and techniques.
3. Use different sentence structures to create different effects, with correct punctuation and spelling.

## Writing to engage the reader

Personal and imaginative writing is everywhere. It is in the emails we send to friends, in blogs and diaries, and in travel accounts in books.

Read the following extract from *Stephen Fry in America,* where the author Stephen Fry writes about swimming with dolphins in Florida. Look carefully at the techniques he uses to engage his readers.

### From *Stephen Fry in America*
**by Stephen Fry**

Although the sheer pleasure of sharing the water with these amiable mammals is reason enough to do it, there has over recent years grown up the practice of Dolphin Therapy. I am due to swim with a boy, Kyle Crouch, who lives with cerebral palsy and has been coming to swim with bottle-nosed dolphins in Key Largo since he was ten years old. A young therapist called Eli has been swimming with him and supervising the sessions and it is clear that they both believe the experience has been wholly beneficial. Kyle's mother agrees.

Annotations:
- amiable: friendly
- I am due to swim: clear explanation of events
- cerebral palsy: a condition which makes movement uncoordinated and jerky
- A young therapist called Eli: details of people and places provide a sense of personal experience
- wholly beneficial: totally good for him

UNIT 1

interesting vocabulary, including lists, helps the reader feel part of the experience

variety of sentence structure and length, with clear punctuation

Maybe it is the sheer exhilaration of being towed, nosed, tickled, slapped, prodded, swiped and barged by the boisterous, squeaking, clicking creatures – maybe that is therapy enough, coupled with the muscular toning resulting from active time in the seawater. I certainly feel enchanted and emerge glowing with *bien-être* and a sense of one of nature's highest privileges having been bestowed upon me.

writer's personality comes through in his description of feelings

well-being

given a special gift

## ACTIVITY 1

Write a blog entry (about 100 words) describing **either** an encounter with an animal **or** an exciting event on holiday. Use some of the writing techniques used in the source text, such as:

- using varied and interesting vocabulary
- showing personality by describing feelings
- including details to help the reader imagine the scene.

## Comparing form and purpose

The extract from a webpage, below, deals with the same sort of experience as Stephen Fry did in his book – swimming with dolphins.

**dolphin days**

**Swim Programmes**

activities where people can meet and swim with dolphins

Dolphin Days offers a variety of dolphin interaction programmes, including Natural Dolphin Swims and Structured Dolphin Swims. These programmes are designed for people interested in learning more about dolphins in a safe, natural seawater environment. In addition to swimming with dolphins, visitors will take part in an educational briefing about dolphin natural history. Our highly trained staff will tell you about dolphin anatomy, social behaviour, reproductive system, echo-location, conservation programmes and what to expect during the swim. Immediately after this, you will experience our amazing in-water programme with dolphins: something you will remember for the rest of your life!

a lesson

the structure of the body

using sound to move around effectively

During our Natural Dolphin Swims, individuals will enter the water with masks, flippers and snorkels to participate in an open swimming session with dolphins. There is no direct contact between swimmers and dolphins during these sessions. This is a truly unique experience, which simulates swimming with dolphins in the wild.

copies

Our Structured Dolphin Swims are close dolphin encounters, during which each swimmer will participate in a variety of trained behaviours (for example, belly rubs, dorsal tows and kisses) with our dolphins. These activities are mediated by an experienced dolphin trainer to ensure the best experience for dolphins and visitors.

rides while holding on to the dolphin's back fin

supervised

## ACTIVITY 2

Copy and complete this grid to compare the text on Pages 34–35 with the text on Page 36. Although both texts deal with the experience of swimming with dolphins, each text is written in a different form and for a different purpose.

Where possible, find quotations to back up your points in the grid.

| Feature | Stephen Fry in America | Dolphin Days |
|---|---|---|
| type of text and audience | travel writing aimed at everyone | website aimed at people who want to swim with dolphins |
| purpose | | to inform and persuade |
| organization/structure | | hyperlinks connect to different parts of the website, e.g. 'Natural Dolphin Swims' |
| specialist vocabulary | no specialist words related to the experience, but a variety of words to interest the reader, e.g. 'amiable' and 'enchanted' | |
| The narrative voice (use of first person 'I', second person 'you' or third person 'he/she/it') | | written mainly in the second and third person, e.g. 'you will experience...' and 'visitors will...' |
| use of facts/opinions | mix of facts and opinions | |
| focus on personal experience | | mention of trained staff makes the reader confident that it would be good |
| how easy it is to understand | written in a friendly style, but using some unusual words, e.g. 'bien-être' | |

## Style, form and vocabulary

You can improve your writing by reading. This will help you to get used to different types of writing and to increase your vocabulary. Try to read everyday texts, such as newspapers, magazines, websites and advertisements.

### FUNCTIONAL SKILLS TASK

**a** Explore different types of writing by researching tourism in your local area, or elsewhere. You could look:
- at leaflets from a Tourist Information Centre
- on the Internet, typing in 'tourism' and the area in a search engine
- for blogs about your chosen area.

**b** With a partner or small group, look at the range of texts you have found. For each text, decide:
- what type of text it is
- what its main purpose is; for example, to advertise, to inform or to entertain.

**c** Draw a spider diagram for each text showing its style, form and key features. Use the questions in the diagram below to help you.

**d** Put the texts in order of how well they meet their purpose, with the best at the top and the worst at the bottom. Not everyone will agree, but talk about your choices.

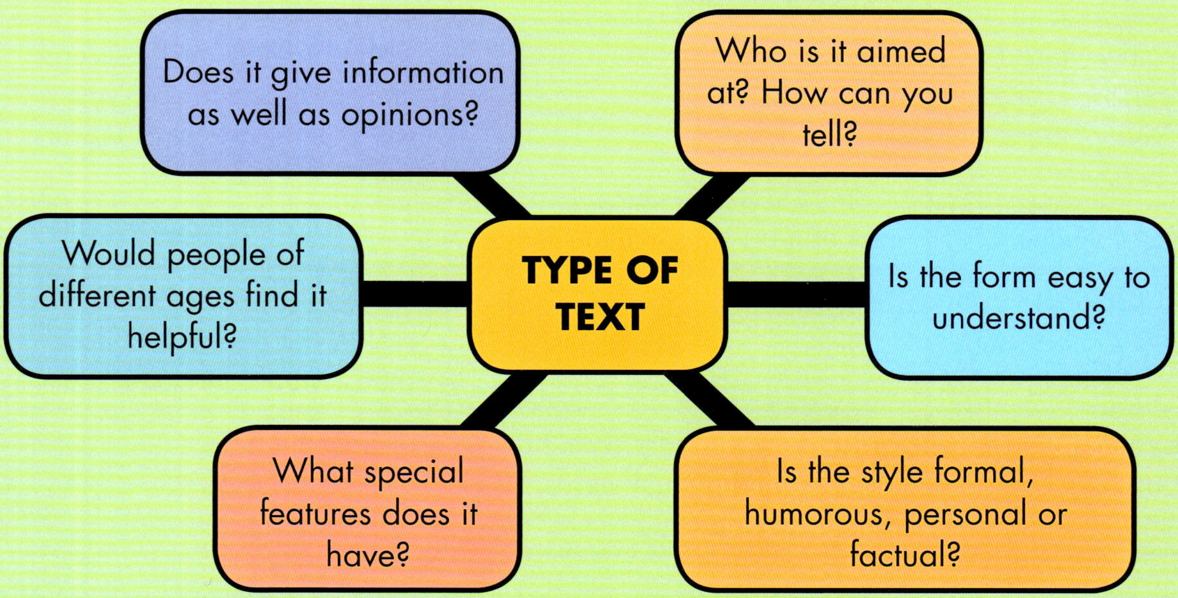

## Widening vocabulary

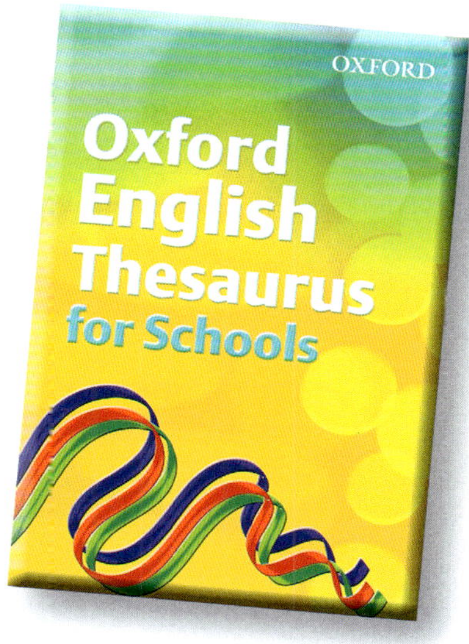


One way of making your writing personal and imaginative is to choose your vocabulary carefully. This can help the reader to understand you and what you feel. When Stephen Fry writes that he feels 'enchanted', he is showing the reader what an emotional effect swimming with dolphins had on him. 'Enchanted' makes the experience sound magical.

Words can build up a balanced picture of an experience. For example, Stephen Fry describes being 'towed, nosed, tickled, slapped, prodded, swiped and barged' by the dolphins which shows us playful, slightly naughty creatures. However, if the first three verbs were missed out, the tone would change and the dolphins would appear to be aggressive.

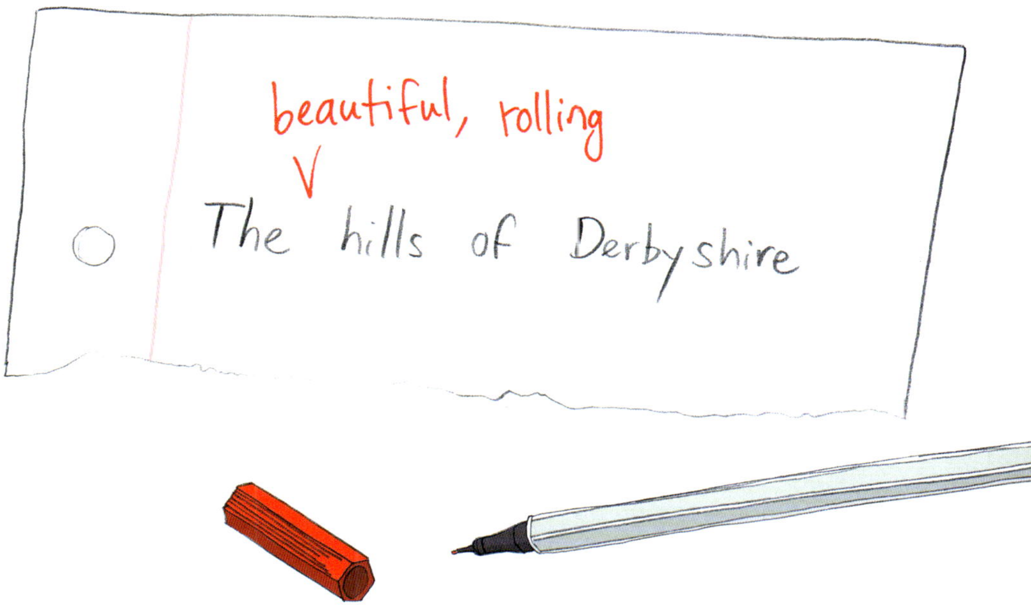


Use a thesaurus to improve your writing. A thesaurus lists synonyms (different words with similar meanings) and gives you the opportunity to try new words.

### ACTIVITY 3

In small groups, choose sentences or phrases from the material you collected about tourism and write each one in the middle of a piece of paper.

Using a thesaurus, add adjectives, adverbs or verbs to change the tone and effect of the sentences. For example, 'the busy centre of Birmingham' could be 'the bustling and lively centre of Birmingham'.

Share some of the best with the rest of the class and discuss the effects created.

## Let your imagination go to work!

On the next two pages are some tasks which will help you to practise your personal and imaginative writing skills. Remember that it is important to plan your work. Use the flow diagram below to remind you of what you need to think about.

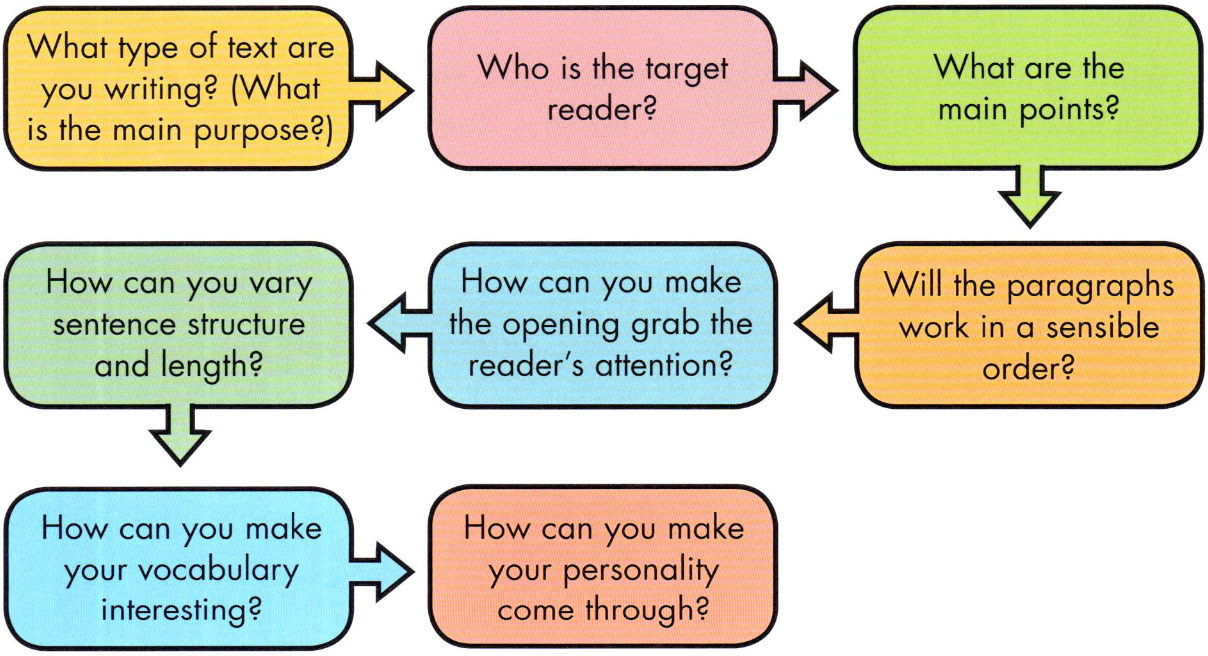




### ACTIVITY 4

**a** Write the text for a leaflet (folded A4 size) encouraging tourists to spend some time in your local area.

- Suggest activities and places to visit. Remember that even a dirty old canal can be 'part of our industrial heritage'!
- Note down what photographs and images you might use to go with the text.
- Think carefully about what effects you would like to create.

**b** Imagine you have visited the Dolphin Days aquatic park (see the webpage about it on Page 36). Write a blog entry of up to 300 words in which you describe your day there.

## ACTIVITY 5

Work in groups to role-play a television programme where people are interviewed about their holiday experiences. The presenter will need to introduce each interview and wrap-up the show at the end. Try to include a mixture of good and bad experiences in your interviews to help make the programme seem realistic.

### *Holidays From Heaven and Hell*

Presenter: Good evening and welcome to *Holidays From Heaven and Hell*. In this episode we will be hearing about a dream holiday in Barbados that turned into a nightmare when…

# Prose Fiction

## LEARNING CHECKLIST

In this chapter you will learn to:

1. Write clearly, with imagination, using a suitable form and words to interest the reader.
2. Write in sentences and paragraphs, using a clear structure and order, and a variety of language features and techniques.
3. Use different sentence structures to create different effects, with correct punctuation and spelling.

AO4

## Using your imagination

In this chapter, you will focus on using your imagination to create texts. These texts will go beyond your personal experience. Look at the spider diagram on the right. It shows some of the key features of prose fiction.

Read the text below. Notice that it has many of the features shown in the spider diagram.

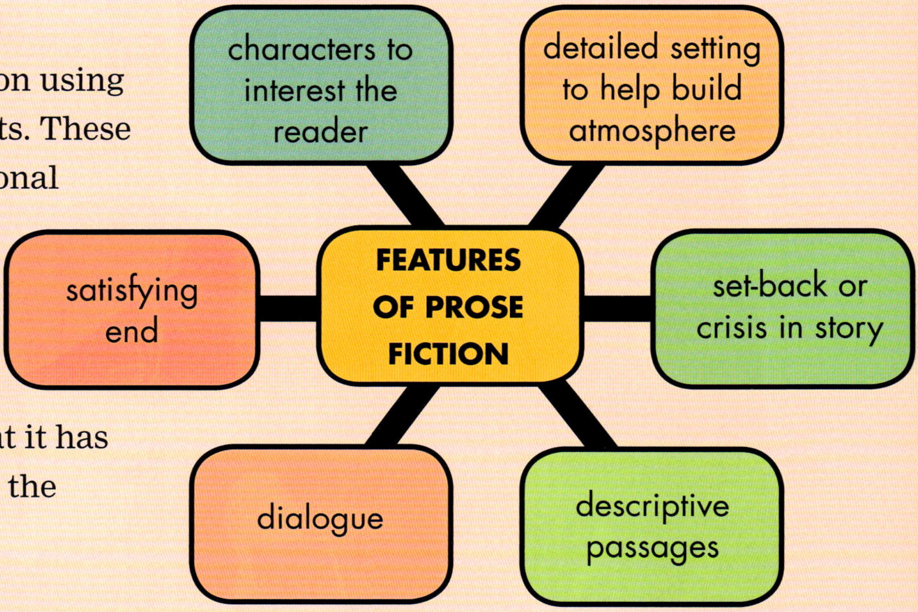


details of the setting

interesting title that tells you what type of story it is

### *Climax for a Ghost Story*

**by I. A. Ireland**

use of varied characters for conflict or contrast

use of speech to move the story on

'How eerie!' said the girl, advancing cautiously. 'And what a heavy door!'. She touched it as she spoke and it suddenly swung to with a click.

'Good Lord!' said the man. 'I don't believe there's a handle inside. Why, you've locked us both in!'

introduction of a crisis to change the way the story will go

'Not both of us. Only one of us,' said the girl, and before his eyes she passed straight through the door and vanished.

an ending that challenges the reader to think

## Identifying genre

In your Controlled Assessment task for this section you will complete one task that has two linked parts. You should aim to entertain your audience and show a range of writing skills.

The examiners will be looking to see how well you can:

- grab and hold the reader's attention
- use a variety of sentences
- use paragraphs to divide up your work
- use interesting vocabulary with correct spellings
- use punctuation.

### ACTIVITY 1

When you plan your writing, you must first think about what genre (type) of story it is. Different genres have different types of characters, settings and plot elements.

**a** In pairs, or small groups, talk about how you would complete the grid on the right.

**b** Choose a genre and plan your own short story.

| Type of story | Type of characters | Type of setting | Plot elements |
|---|---|---|---|
| horror | mysterious characters, ghosts | | |
| fantasy | | | magic spells, epic battles |
| sci-fi | | futuristic or space-based settings | |
| romance | lovers, villains | | |
| adventure | heroic characters, villains | | |

## What makes a good opening?

The most important part of any story is the opening. Read the two story openings on this page and think about:

- how the reader is drawn into the story
- how language is used to interest the reader
- what type or genre each story belongs to.

### From *The Curious Incident of the Dog in the Night-time* by Mark Haddon

It was 7 minutes after midnight. The dog was lying on the grass in the middle of the lawn in front of Mrs Shears' house. Its eyes were closed. It looked as if it was running on its side, the way dogs run when they think they are chasing a cat in a dream. But the dog was not running or asleep. The dog was dead. There was a garden fork sticking out of the dog.



### From *The Chrysalids* by John Wyndham

When I was quite small I would sometimes dream of a city – which was strange because it began even before I knew what a city was. But this city, clustered on the curve of a big blue bay, would come into my mind. I could see the streets, and the buildings that lined them, the waterfront, even boats in the harbour; yet, waking, I had never seen the sea, or a boat…

And the buildings were quite unlike any I knew. The traffic in the streets was strange, carts running with no horses to pull them…

## ACTIVITY 2

Compare the openings on Page 44 using the points below to help you.

- Which of the two opening sentences do you like best? Why?
- Why do you think the other one is weaker? Explain your answer with close reference to the text.
- Which extract gives most information about the **narrator** (the person who tells the story)?

## ACTIVITY 3

Now use what you have learnt so far to write the opening (about 100 words) to an adventure story called 'Lost'.

**a** First, plan your story. Copy and complete the grid to help you:

| Title of story | Type of story | Type of characters | Type of setting | Plot elements |
|---|---|---|---|---|
| Lost | | | | |
| | | | | |
| | | | | |

**b** Write your opening in the centre of your page and leave space around it to highlight and annotate key features.

**c** Annotate your piece of writing to show key features. These might include:

- how you get the reader's interest in the first sentence
- the language you use
- the way you introduce the characters
- how you set the scene.

## Developing settings

To develop a good story, you need more than just action. If you describe the setting, you take your reader into the heart of the story, help create atmosphere and build up tension.

Use this **checklist** to help you describe a setting.

- Think about what effect you want to have on your reader.
- Imagine what the setting looks like in your mind before you describe it.
- Use a thesaurus to find interesting vocabulary.
- Describe sounds, smells, textures as well as sights.

### From *The Season Ticket*
**by Jonathan Tulloch**

Dejectedly they trailed into the park which had been built when Gateshead had played host to the International Garden Festival. The flower beds and walkways were gradually sinking back into the general dereliction of the area but they still retained some of the original grandeur and design. The Dunston Rocket tower block rose above them, its top floors beginning to disappear with the closing weather. It started to rain […]

miserably (Dejectedly)
falling into ruin (dereliction)
kept (retained)
magnificence (grandeur)
clouds gathering in (closing weather)

UNIT 1

**ACTIVITY 4**

**a** Use the checklist on Page 46 to examine how Jonathan Tulloch uses description in *The Season Ticket*.

**b** Discuss how you could change the atmosphere by changing vocabulary. For example, change 'dejectedly' to 'excitedly'.

**c** Write a description of a place you know well as it might appear in a story. Before you write, decide what **type** of story it is going to fit into; for example a horror story, a romance or something else.

The worst thing he/she ever did was...

His/her voice is...

The thing he/she hates most is...

The best thing about him/her is...

I always think of him/her wearing...

## Building character

To create believable characters you need to have a clear idea of them in your own head. Imagine how they:

- look
- behave
- think
- respond to other characters.

You also need to think carefully about how to put them across to your readers. Below are some suggestions.

- Use comparisons (similes and metaphors) to describe them. These can give clues about their personalities. For example, if you describe a character 'with a voice like ice', you are also hinting that they are cold and sharp.
- Try to use appearance to show something about your character's mood or personality. For example: 'His tie was loose and there were black marks on his shirt. His eyes were large and dazed.'
- If your character speaks, make sure that what the character says matches his or her personality.

**ACTIVITY 5**

Create two characters for your story 'Lost', which you planned on Page 45. One character should be a hero, the other a villain.

**a** First write some notes about your characters. Use the speech bubbles above to help trigger ideas.

**b** Decide on names that suit the setting and story type.

**c** Write a paragraph about each character. Try to show their personalities through what they say and do.

## Using dialogue

You will need to include some dialogue (speech) in your story. The extract below shows the rules for speech layout.

Emily approached the man behind the counter and held up the photograph that was clutched in her hand. 'Have you seen this girl? I think she works here.'

'No,' replied the man, 'I don't recognize her.'

'Are you sure?' Emily asked. 'I was told that this is where she works – the High Street Cafe.'

When the man firmly shook his head again, she sighed dejectedly and turned to leave.

use a new line for a new speaker

separate the words in speech marks from the rest of the sentence with a comma, exclamation mark or question mark

the first word inside speech marks begins with a capital letter

the words actually spoken go inside the speech marks

Dialogue can be used to:

- add humour
- explain feelings or events
- increase tension
- show more about the character
- help move the story on

### ACTIVITY 6

With a partner, write a short conversation between the two characters you created for Activity 5 on Page 47. Be prepared to explain how the dialogue moves the story on or reveals something about the characters.

## Writing a story

Now practise the skills you have developed in this chapter by writing your own story in the activities below.

### ACTIVITY 7

Write a story called 'The Big Change'.

**a** Plan your story using a spider diagram or flow chart to map ideas for settings, characters and twists in the plot.

**b** Write your story. Remember to vary your language and sentence structure to give variety.

### ACTIVITY 8

Choose one of the activities below. They all relate to your story 'The Big Change'.

- Write a preview of a film version of your story.
- Write a series of emails between two of your characters about events in the story.
- Write a newspaper report about one of the events.

## SECTION B: IMAGINATIVE WRITING

### How can I plan for the Imaginative Writing task?

You are allowed to plan in pairs or groups – your teacher will advise you what to do. You should look at examples of other people's writing. This will help you to understand what makes a good piece of imaginative writing. You will be given time in class to practise before the final assessment.

By the time you go into the Controlled Assessment, you should have a clear idea of what you are going to write and how you are going to write it.

### What should the style be?

Make sure that you read the wording of the tasks carefully. This will help you to work out what style you need to use. Think about these factors:

- **Form:** What type of writing is it? Is it a script, a piece of description or a story? Or is it something else?
- **Purpose:** What is the writing for? Is it to inform or to persuade or to entertain? Or is there some other purpose? Remember that one piece of writing can have more than one purpose.
- **Audience:** Who is the writing for? Is it for adults or children? Is it for people with a specific interest?

## How much should I write?

You should write about 1200 words for both tasks added together, about 600 words for each one. Writing more than necessary will not gain you any extra marks. You should focus on the quality of your writing rather than aiming to write pages and pages.

## What are controlled conditions?

- There will be a time limit of **four hours** to complete both tasks.
- You are allowed to type your answer but you are not allowed to use a spelling or grammar checker, or the Internet.
- You may take brief bullet-pointed notes into the assessment, but no other paperwork.
- You have to do the final piece of work on your own, without help from your teacher or anyone else.

# Unit 2

## Speaking, Listening and Spoken Language

## HOW TO APPROACH UNIT 2

### What will I cover in this unit?

This unit is divided into two sections:

- **Section A** tests speaking and listening.
- **Section B** tests how well you can comment on the use of spoken language.

### How will the speaking and listening tasks be assessed?

You will be assessed in three tasks:

- an individual presentation
- a group activity
- a drama-focused activity.

### How will the spoken language task be assessed?

You can choose to look at **Part A** or **Part B**.

**Part A:** This is a study of the spoken language of a public figure (such as a politician) or an interviewer (such as Michael Parkinson).

**Part B:** you can look at one of the following topics:

- Language, Media and Technology, including the study of a TV programme
- Language and Society.

Whether you do Part A or Part B, you can link this activity to one of your speaking and listening assessments.

## SECTION A: SPEAKING AND LISTENING

### What will the tasks be like?

Throughout your course you will take part in both formal and informal speaking and listening activities.

One of the activities that you will be assessed on must be based on a real-life situation that could take place outside of the classroom, for example, presenting an idea for a new video game to a software company.

### What will I be marked on?

You will be marked on Assessment Objective 1, which covers the skills listed below.

- Speak clearly and to the point; change your talk to suit different situations and audiences; use Standard English and a range of techniques.
- Listen to speakers and respond to what they say with your own comments, ideas and points of view.
- Work with others, using comments and questions to pull ideas together.
- Take on different roles.

Each speaking and listening task is worth **40 marks**. Once each task has been marked, the marks will be added together and divided by three to give an average mark out of 40. These tasks are worth **20%** of the total marks for your English Language GCSE.

# 2.1 Individual Contribution

**LEARNING CHECKLIST**

In this chapter you will learn to:

1 Speak clearly and to the point.

2 Adapt talk to different situations and audiences.

3 Use Standard English.

AO1

## Planning a presentation

As part of your speaking and listening assessment, you may be asked to plan a speech or presentation before delivering it to an audience. To be successful, you must think about **what** you are going to say and **how** you are going to say it before you actually give your speech.

Plan your speech, dividing it into three steps.

- **Step 1:** greet your audience and introduce the title of the talk, explaining what it is about.
- **Step 2:** give the key information in a clear order.
- **Step 3:** sum up your ideas and invite questions.

Good morning. My intention is to persuade you, Mr Jones, that abolishing homework would be beneficial to students' education and well-being.

**ACTIVITY 1**

Imagine that you have five minutes to persuade your English teacher to stop giving you homework. Read the speech bubbles and answer the questions below.

**a** Which would be the least appropriate way to begin?

**b** Which would be the most appropriate way to begin?

**c** Explain your choices. Try to use the terms: 'Standard English', 'formal', 'informal' and 'colloquial'.

Alright mate. Look, we've had enough of this homework business...

Dearest teacher, I stand before you today a student struggling under the burden of hours of homework...

## Presenting persuasively

If the aim of your presentation is to persuade your audience to do or think something, then you need to use **persuasive language**. The extract below is from a speech given in assembly by a student trying to persuade others that they need a new school uniform.

Good morning fellow students. I am here to talk to you about the issue of school uniform. Have you ever looked in the mirror and thought, my school uniform looks really cool? How about wearing it out on a Friday night? I thought not.

If we are forced to wear a uniform, at least it should be remotely fashionable. We are one of only 27% of schools in the entire country where students still have to endure a tie. There are millions of schools where pupils' uniforms are modern, comfortable and, dare I say, vaguely stylish. Enough is enough: we don't expect designer gear, but this dreary, drab and dreadful dress code has to go!

### ACTIVITY 2

Read the extract and copy and complete the grid below.

| Persuasive technique | Example from the speech | Why this is persuasive |
|---|---|---|
| rhetorical questions | | |
| use of facts or figures | 'one of only 27% of schools' | This is the minority so it should be changed. |
| rule of three | 'modern, comfortable and, dare I say, vaguely stylish' | |
| humour | | |
| use of pronouns, such as 'I', 'you' and 'we' | | |

### FUNCTIONAL SKILLS TASK

FUNCTIONAL SKILLS

You have been asked to speak at the local leisure centre to persuade the management to provide three new activities for teenagers. These could include after-school clubs or trips. In your presentation, remember to:

- introduce yourself and explain the purpose of your presentation
- outline three new activities that you would introduce and explain why
- use formal language.

# Group Activity

**LEARNING CHECKLIST**

In this chapter you will learn to:

1 Listen and respond to other people's ideas.

2 Use suggestions, comments and questions to pull ideas together.

AO1

## Listening carefully

When you work in a group, it is important that you listen carefully to what other people are saying.

### ACTIVITY 1

**a** Why is it important to listen to the other members of your group?

**b** What might happen if you don't listen carefully during a discussion?

**c** Copy and complete the spider diagram on the right. Add other actions that can show that you are listening.

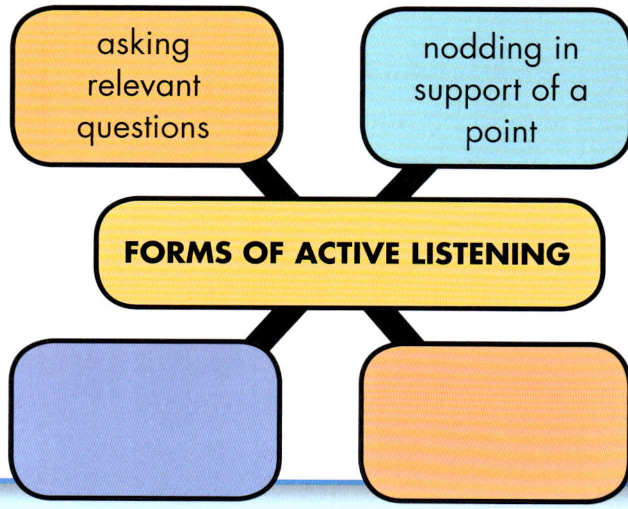


### ACTIVITY 2

In pairs, spend two minutes telling your partner about your weekend.

**a** As the first person talks, the second should respond as a **bad** listener might.

**b** Swap over so that the second person talks and the first person responds as a **good** listener might.

**c** Discuss the points below.
- How did it feel to talk to a bad listener?
- How did your partner show you that he or she was listening well?

## Responding appropriately

In your assessment you will be given marks for how well you respond to what others say. This would be important in a job interview, for example, where you would need to give detailed answers and use formal language.

### FUNCTIONAL SKILLS TASK

You are part of the production team for the TV show *Teentastic!* and you are looking for a new presenter to host the show. Read the personal specification for this job, below:

> **Personal specification**
>
> Candidates must be:
>
> - confident at presenting to camera
> - able to work well both independently and as part of a team
> - fun, with a bubbly personality and an excellent sense of humour
> - willing to take on plenty of exciting challenges from fire-eating to bungee jumping!

**a** In your group, write a list of ten questions that you will ask the candidates for this job at interview.

- Use formal language in your questions and in the discussion.
- Make sure that you ask questions about everything in the personal specification.
- Make sure the questions need detailed answers.
- Listen to each other and try to get everyone involved.

**b** Get together with another group and take it in turns to interview each other. As each person is interviewed, rate:

- how well he or she listens to the questions
- how detailed and appropriate his or her responses are.

**c** Give each candidate advice on how to improve their interview technique in order to win that job!

# 2.3 Drama

## LEARNING CHECKLIST

AO1

In this chapter you will learn to:

1 Listen and respond to speakers' ideas, points of view and expression.
2 Use suggestions, comments and questions to pull ideas together.
3 Take on different roles during activities.

## Taking on a role

When you take on the role of a character, you need to think carefully about how that character thinks and feels and how he or she shows this. This means that you need to think about **what** your character might say and **how** he or she might say it.

## ACTIVITY 1

Imagine you live in a village where there has been a proposal to hold a three-day music festival. You are going to take on the roles of various members of the village.

**a** Discuss who might be affected by the proposal, for example, shopkeepers, farmers, elderly people or teenagers.

**b** Work in groups of four. Each person decides what role to play. Then the group should act out a conversation where they discuss what they think about the festival idea. You could imagine that this takes place in a local café or shop.

## Using actions as well as words

While you are talking in role, think carefully about your facial expressions and **body language**. Even if you are not moving or saying anything, you can still show your character by the way you stand and behave.

### ACTIVITY 2

Imagine the village calls a meeting to discuss the festival. Improvise the cebate with the whole class.

**a** Decide who is going to be:

- the chairperson
- the festival organizer
- a local councillor
- a police representative
- a youth club leader
- a local shopkeeper
- anyone else you can think of.

**b** In the debate, take turns to put forward your views, listening carefully to each other and responding to the points made.

**c** At the end of the debate take a vote on whether the festival should go ahead.

# PREPARING FOR UNIT 2

## SECTION A: SPEAKING AND LISTENING

### How can I plan for my assessment?

Thinking about the following points will help you to carry out your speaking and listening tasks well:

- **Identifying your audience.** You will gain marks if you show that you have thought about who your talk is for. You can do this by choosing the right kinds of words and the right style of speech.
- **Listening to others.** You must show that you can listen to other people and answer their questions or reply to their ideas in a group task.
- **Creating and sustaining different roles.** Think carefully about your character before the assessment.

### How long will the assessments take?

You will do three speaking and listening tasks. For each one, you will need between three and five lessons, including some discussion with your teacher before you are assessed.

**Remember**, discussion is about listening to others as well as speaking!

# HOW TO APPROACH UNIT 2

## SECTION B: SPOKEN LANGUAGE

### What will the tasks be like?

For this section, you have a choice of activities. You can choose either:

**Part A:** the study of the Spoken Language of a Public Figure, which will be the study of a particular speaker or of a particular interviewer.
**Or**
**Part B:** the study of Language, Media and Technology or Language and Society.

Language, Media and Technology will include the study of a TV programme. Language and Society may include the study of how men and women use language, how spoken language has changed over time or how people speak differently in different situations.

### Can my speaking and listening work relate to these tasks?

Yes. Your presentation, group work or drama-focused work can be linked to your spoken language assessment. Your teacher will advise you.

### Is there a word limit?

You must complete your Controlled Assessment as a written essay of approximately **1000 words**.

# 2.4 Spoken Language of a Public Figure

**LEARNING CHECKLIST**

In this chapter you will learn to:

1 Understand how spoken language changes to suit different situations.

2 Judge the effect of your own and others' spoken language.

AO2

## Differences between spoken and written language

You might think that spoken language is the same as written language, except that one is heard and the other is visible, but you would be wrong! There are many important differences.

### ACTIVITY 1

Find a two-minute extract of speech online. It could be a clip from a TV programme or a radio show. Write down exactly what is said. Then look at a printed page from a novel. What differences are there between the spoken and written language used in these examples? Copy and complete a grid like the one on the right.

| Points to consider | Spoken language | Written language |
| --- | --- | --- |
| How many people are involved? | | |
| Does the writer/speaker pause or hesitate? | | |
| Can you identify evidence of sounds that are not words? | | |
| Does the speaker/writer use full sentences? | | |

UNIT 2

## Planning and creating speech

Most spoken language is created instantly, in response to what's happening and as part of a conversation. People generally speak without much chance to plan, which means it is **spontaneous**.

### ACTIVITY 2

List three conversations you have had in the last few days. For each one, write down:

**a** how many people were involved

**b** how much planning was involved. Use a scale of 1–5, with 5 being the most spontaneous.

## Public and private speech

In this chapter, you will focus on the spoken language of a public figure. Most public figures have what they say broadcast in the media, such as on the radio, TV and websites. Their audiences are often large and mixed, so they have to make sure that what they say interests as many people as possible.

One of your assessment tasks for this unit is to study the spoken language of either a particular speaker or an interviewer. You will need to think carefully about how this type of spoken language is different from everyday talk.

### ACTIVITY 3

Read the examples in the speech bubbles below. With a partner, decide which might be spoken by a public figure on a public occasion and which might be spoken by family or friends in private. Some of them might be both. Give your reasons by completing a grid like the one below.

| Example speech | Public | Private | Both | Why? |
|---|---|---|---|---|
| We, as a nation, cannot and will not let our most vulnerable suffer like this... | ✔ | | | Because it says 'we as a nation' which makes it sound like a big formal event. It sounds like a speech to a whole country. |
| Hey, did you hear how rude she was to her so-called boyfriend? | | | | |
| Please explain to our viewers why you want to abolish schools. | | | | |
| Don't tell anyone but... | | | | |

## Appealing to the audience

All public speakers need to think carefully about their audiences. Politicians and campaigners try to make the audience feel important and persuade them that he or she is 'on their side'.

In contrast, an interviewer needs to speak on behalf of the audience, asking questions and finding out information from the interviewee. An interviewer has to make the listeners feel valued and at the same time develop a relationship with the person that he/she is interviewing.

Read the transcripts of spoken language on this page. **Transcript 1** is the opening of a political campaign speech by Barack Obama. **Transcript 2** shows the opening words of a host on a TV chat show.

**1**

'Let me begin by saying thanks to all you who've travelled, from far and wide, to brave the cold today.

We all made this journey for a reason. It's humbling, but in my heart I know you didn't come here just for me, you came here because you believe in what this country can be.'

- *thanks to all you* – shows that he appreciates his audience
- *We all made this journey* – use of 'we' shows that he is one of them
- *humbling* – makes him feel unworthy of such attention
- *I know you didn't come here just for me* – shows that he is modest
- *you believe in what this country can be* – encourages audience to feel they can achieve great things if they work together

**2**

'Good evening. Thank you for joining me again for another chance to put today's most pressing questions to the country's leaders. I hope that together we can explore the controversial action being taken on our children's schools. Please join me in welcoming the Minister of State for Schools and Learners...'

- *controversial* – something which people don't agree on

### ACTIVITY 4

Look at **Transcript 1**. It has been annotated to show how Barack Obama establishes a relationship with his audience. Now look at **Transcript 2**. Annotate it to show how the speaker:

- builds a relationship with the audience
- begins to build a relationship with his guest.

## Pace, pauses and body language

When speakers prepare a speech, they have to think about **how** they will speak as well as **what** they are going to say. Here are some **non-verbal** (unspoken) aspects of speech-making that you could comment on:

- how fast or slow the speech is
- how often the speaker pauses
- how loud or quiet the speaker is
- how much eye contact he or she makes with the audience
- body language (the way the speaker stands or uses his or her hands).

When you write about speech, you need to think about how these things affect the way an audience might react. If a speaker slows the pace of speech down, this can help people to hear the words more clearly and add emphasis. Speeding up a speech can add more energy and excitement.

A carefully placed pause can give the audience more time to think about the point that has just been made. Movement and body language can help make the meaning clearer but too much can be distracting.

### ACTIVITY 5

In small groups, take turns to present the opening of the speech about football that appears on the right of this page.

**a** On your first turn, deliberately get one of the non-verbal skills listed on this page wrong. For example, you might speak too quietly, too fast or use too many pauses. The rest of the group then has to spot the flaw in your speech.

**b** On your second turn, present the speech effectively. The rest of the group should then comment on what you did well.

'How many people do you know who love football? I'm betting that everyone knows someone with a passion for "the beautiful game". You may even have the passion yourself. Football is more than a game, it's a national obsession.'

## Rhetoric: the art of speech-making

The sound and rhythm of a speech can have a powerful effect on an audience.

'Rhetoric' is the Greek term for the art of speech-making. Public speakers use a variety of **rhetorical devices** to add impact to their words. Here are some common devices:

- **emotive words**, for example: 'our brave lads' rather than 'the soldiers'
- **rhetorical questions**, for example: 'Do you find this acceptable?'
- **balanced phrases**, for example: 'to work and to live'
- **antithesis** or placing opposite meanings together, for example: 'Let us shape our hopelessness into new hope'
- **repetition**, for example: 'We will stand up, we will fight, we will win.'
- **groups of three**, for example: 'Friends, Romans, countrymen'
- **alliteration**, for example: 'a tapestry of talents'.



### ACTIVITY 6

Read the transcript of the opening of Obama's nomination speech on Page 67. Find examples of rhetorical devices and comment on the effect upon the audience. Some have already been highlighted to help you. Think about whether the devices:

- stir up emotion
- make something memorable
- give emphasis
- encourage people to take action.

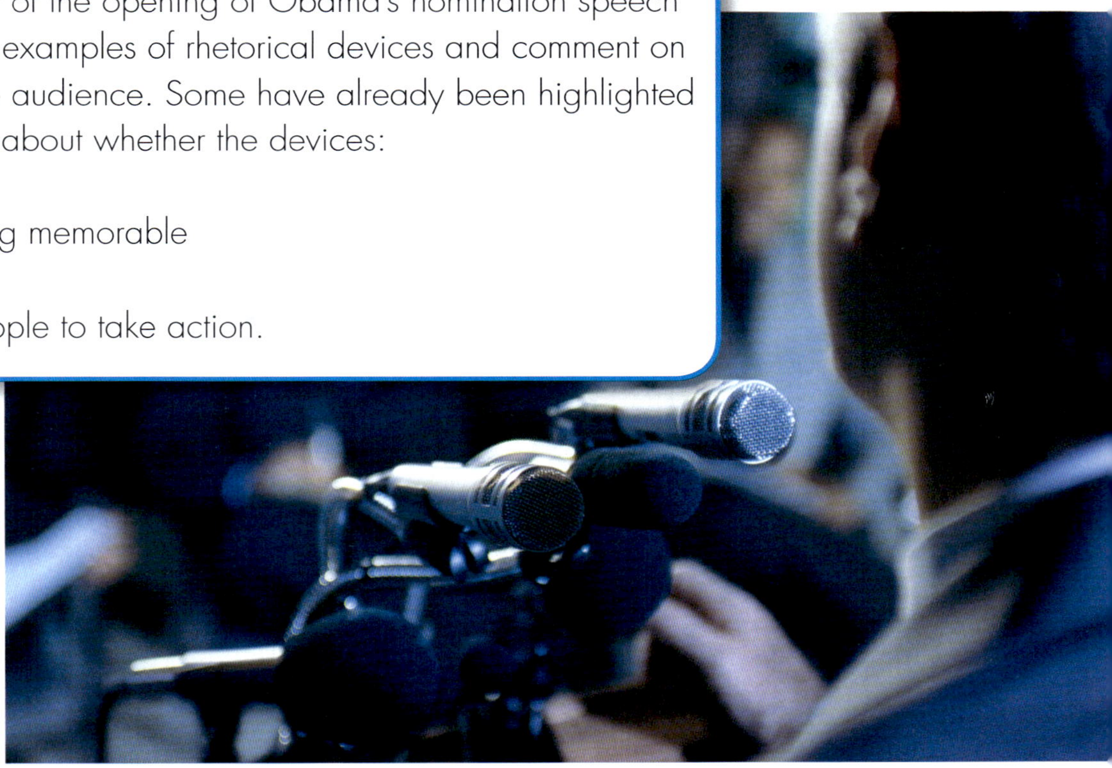

Here is the opening of Barack Obama's campaign speech for nomination for US President.

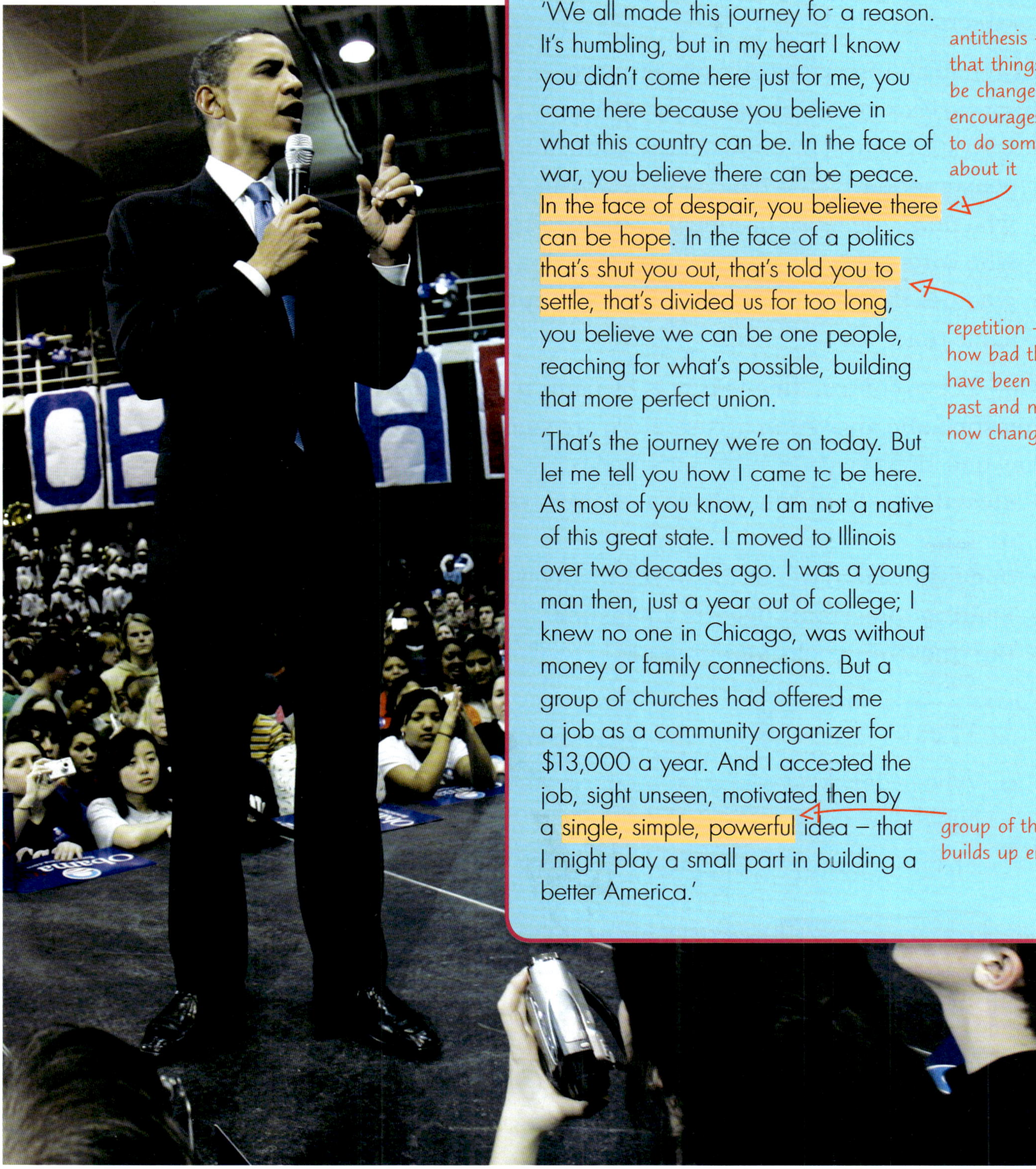


'Let me begin by saying thanks to all you who've travelled, from far and wide, to brave the cold today.

'We all made this journey for a reason. It's humbling, but in my heart I know you didn't come here just for me, you came here because you believe in what this country can be. In the face of war, you believe there can be peace. In the face of despair, you believe there can be hope. In the face of a politics that's shut you out, that's told you to settle, that's divided us for too long, you believe we can be one people, reaching for what's possible, building that more perfect union.

antithesis – shows that things can be changed and encourages people to do something about it

repetition – shows how bad things have been in the past and must now change

'That's the journey we're on today. But let me tell you how I came to be here. As most of you know, I am not a native of this great state. I moved to Illinois over two decades ago. I was a young man then, just a year out of college; I knew no one in Chicago, was without money or family connections. But a group of churches had offered me a job as a community organizer for $13,000 a year. And I accepted the job, sight unseen, motivated then by a single, simple, powerful idea – that I might play a small part in building a better America.'

group of three – builds up emphasis

## Techniques of interviewing

For your assessment task you may study a particular interviewer. If so, you will need to look at how the interviewer controls other speakers.

Listen to an interview with one or more interviewees and think carefully about:

- who speaks first or **chooses the topic** for the conversation
- who takes the most, or longest, **turns** to speak
- who **interrupts**
- whether the speakers **overlap** and talk at the same time.

One way to control turn-taking is by using a question and answer structure. Here are some key question types:

- **closed question:** can only be answered 'yes' or 'no'
- **open question:** can be answered in any way
- **leading question:** suggests an answer
- **tag question:** looks for agreement.

### ACTIVITY 7

**a** What types of questions are shown in the speech bubbles here? Use the list above to help you.

**b** What sort of response is each one likely to get?

UNIT 2

## Sir Michael Parkinson

Sir Michael Parkinson is one of the most famous interviewers on TV and radio in the UK. He has interviewed almost 1000 of the world's most famous people.

You can watch many of Parkinson's interviews on his website. Some of Parkinson's most famous guests included Nelson Mandela, Will Smith, Gwyneth Paltrow, Sir Paul McCartney, David Beckham, Simon Cowell, Tom Cruise, Sanjeev Bhaskar and David Tennant.

### ACTIVITY 8

Watch two of Parkinson's interviews in detail. In pairs, copy and complete the grid below.

| Points to consider | Interview 1 | Interview 2 |
|---|---|---|
| the way Parkinson introduces his guest to the audience before he or she appears | | |
| how he greets his guest – what he says and what he does | | |
| use of humour | | |
| how Parkinson shows respect for his guest | | |
| Parkinson's body language, such as eye contact, hand movements and facial expressions | | |
| the style of questions that Parkinson asks | | |
| how Parkinson rounds off the interview at the end and thanks his guest | | |

# 2.5 Language, Media and Technology

**LEARNING CHECKLIST**

In this chapter you will learn to:

1 Understand how spoken language changes to suit different situations.

2 Judge the effect of your own and others' spoken language.

AO2

## Recording and broadcasting speech

With today's technology, you probably hear more spoken language through digital media such as TV, MP3 players and mobile phones than in live, face-to-face talk.

Spoken language used in the media is recorded and broadcast to the public. Most everyday face-to-face talk is likely to stay private. People change how they talk depending on the situations they are in. For example, if people know that they are being recorded, they tend to think more carefully about what they say.

### ACTIVITY 1

In pairs, think of examples of spoken language that you have listened to recently via media and technology. Decide whether each example is **scripted** (written down), **unscripted** or a mixture of the two.

Use a grid, like the one started on the right. Think about different media sources such as TV, radio and the Internet.

| Scripted | Unscripted | Mixture |
|---|---|---|
| TV drama, e.g. Hollyoaks | TV talk shows, e.g. Jeremy Kyle | TV reality shows, e.g. The Apprentice |
| radio... | | |

In this chapter you will study unscripted spoken language and how it varies in the media, through the use of technology and in face-to-face situations.



UNIT 2

## Editing broadcasts

'Reality' shows are popular on TV. However, they do not simply record 'real' talk. Most programmes mix different types of spoken language from a variety of speakers. Here are some types of talk you might find in a reality show:

- **voice-over:** scripted commentary from an unseen presenter
- **voice piece to camera:** a regular presenter delivering semi-scripted or planned speech
- **interview:** between the presenter and guest(s), where the presenter has questions prepared
- **conversation:** unscripted, but edited, talk between two or more people
- **vox pop:** edited highlights from various people talking on a single topic.

With the use of technology, editors can change what the viewer gets to hear. They choose the most interesting or controversial parts, and put them together to make the show entertaining.

### ACTIVITY 2

Choose a reality TV programme. As you watch it:

**a** note down the different types of spoken language used

**b** for each type of spoken language that you identify, note how much planning you think it needed.

The grid shows an example taken from *Big Brother*, a reality show on UK TV. In this TV show, contestants lived in a house and were filmed continuously. Each week, the general public voted contestants out of the house. The last one left was the winner.

| Big Brother Eviction Night | Degree of planning (1–10) |
|---|---|
| title music and visuals | 10 |
| voice piece to camera | 9 |
| voice-over 1 | 10 |
| conversation 1 | 4 |
| voice-over 2 | 10 |
| conversation 2 | 5 |
| interview | 6 |

## Language patterns

Many media programmes use set language patterns that are repeated in each episode. These may be expressions that are used time and time again, for example, words used by reporters to open and close news stories.

Some media shows also use **catch phrases**. These short, repeated expressions are easy for people to remember and help to create a brand for the programme. Some catch phrases are linked with sound effects, animations or images to help them stick in the audience's mind. For example, in the BBC's reality TV show *The Apprentice*, Alan Sugar's catch phrase 'You're fired' is always said with an image of his pointing finger.

### ACTIVITY 3

With a partner:

**a** Jot down as many catch phrases as you can think of from programmes that you have seen or heard.

**b** Discuss whether these catch phrases are used in spoken language outside the programme.

## Conventions in conversation

When we speak, we use patterns of language which are predictable. People often try to match the **level of formality**, so 'Good morning' is likely to get 'Good morning' in return, but 'Hi' would get a more informal response.

The speech bubbles on the right show common pairs of spoken exchanges.

Question and answer pairs are predictable because an answer is generally expected in response to a question. Some questions are **open** and might get a variety of responses. **Closed** questions are likely to get a short and predictable answer.

I'm so sorry.

That's alright.

Thank you.

It's a pleasure.

Your hair looks great.

Thanks.

Please come to my party.

I'd love to/I'm afraid I can't.

## ACTIVITY 4

**a** Decide whether the questions below are open or closed.

'Is there any chance of lending me a fiver?'

'Lovely day, isn't it?'

'Do you like my new haircut?'

'Why didn't you tell me she was coming?'

'What are you doing this weekend?'

'Have you got a minute?'

**b** Write down possible answers to the questions. Compare your answers with a partner. Are there any similarities?

## Hostile questioning

Media presenters may ask some straightforward questions simply to seek information from their guests, but other questions may be loaded. **Loaded questions** try to provoke a certain reaction. This type of question is often used to try to reveal the underlying attitude of the speaker. **Hostile questions** are asked to provoke an emotional response from the speaker. They are often used in political interviews.

### ACTIVITY 5

Look at the questions below. Which ones do you think are loaded? What might the speaker be implying in each case?

'Do you think that constant fighting is good for your child?'

'Why don't you leave him?'

'So, do you really think you can compare yourself to...?'

'What's the name of your new album?'

'How well did you know each other before you got married?'

'Didn't you stop to consider the consequences?'

## Power and status

The relationship between a professional broadcaster and a member of the public is usually unequal. The presenter has more control because it is his or her show, but some members of the public manage to stand up for themselves. They can do this by using strategies such as:

- **partial agreement:** 'you have a point... but...'
- **reframing the question:** 'it is not about leaving him...'
- **calmly restating the point:** 'I *have* considered the consequences.'

## Linked responses

It is not only question and answer pairs that can be predictable. In many conversations in the media, one person will respond to a statement by repeating key words; for example, '50,000 spectators!' or by encouraging further explanation, using a phrase such as 'Tell me more.'

**Linguists** (experts in language) believe that most conversations follow set patterns and conventions. This has been tested by programming a computer with the 'rules' of conversation and asking volunteers to have a conversation with it.

The computer is able to follow the 'rules' of conversation, such as question and answer exchanges, matching the level of formality and reassuring the speaker that it has understood statements by repeating words that the speaker has used.

### ACTIVITY 6

Although computers can follow the rules of speech, in real life these rules are sometimes broken. How might the following events change the conventions of speech?

- One speaker mishears the other speaker.
- One speaker is uncomfortable with the topic of conversation.

## Features of unscripted language

When people are talking without a script or without much planning, their language is likely to have certain features which are so common you probably don't notice them.

Here are some examples:

| Features of unscripted language | Examples |
|---|---|
| repetition | 'I will add, I will add' |
| incomplete sentences | 'it was just... I don't know' |
| backchannel behaviour (where the listener uses sounds and words to show that they're listening) | 'yeah/mmm/right' |
| fillers | 'y' know/I mean' |
| vague language | 'sort of/whatever' |
| intensifiers | 'just/really/actually' |



### ACTIVITY 7

Read the transcript from a radio show on Page 77.

**a** List the speakers and rate how much planning each speaker is likely to have had. Use a scale of 1–10, where 10 is the highest amount of planning.

**b** Pick out features of unscripted language in the transcript. A few have already been highlighted for you.

This radio phone-in includes the following:

- presenter promoting the programme
- sound effects (SFX), including a pre-recorded jingle
- presenter introducing the caller
- interaction: presenter's speech
- interaction: caller's speech
- presenter's links to other speakers
- speaker presenting the weather, traffic and news.

**Presenter:** It's 6pm and we're live with a roundup of this week's football action.

This is yours truly, Gareth Newman, waiting for your calls every weeknight from six 'til seven. Call 0123 456789 or text us on 1123.

Radio Newport (SFX) – your favourite radio station.

We'll be bringing you all the latest news from the terraces, plus reports from news and travel every 15 minutes...

But first let's go to Lisa with the latest traffic news. Lisa?

**Lisa:** Hi Gareth. Yes... er, traffic's flowing pretty steadily in the city centre, but there's a bit of a hold-up between Junctions 9 and 10... It's very slow, so avoid it if at all possible.

filler

**Presenter:** We'll bring you an update in a few minutes time, after the news.

Meanwhile... we've got, uh, Danny on Line One. How're you doing, Danny?

**Danny:** Not so bad, Gareth.

**Presenter:** So, what's your point today?

**Danny:** Well, erm, I'm just hoping the back four put in a better performance tonight, really.

**Presenter:** Yeah, I can see what you're saying... I quite like Turner, to be honest.

**Danny:** Yeah. Yeah, you've definitely got a point there... I mean, obviously.

**Presenter:** OK, thank you. That's Danny, a United fan from Moorside...

We've got literally hundreds of texts coming in but let's get back to the lines.

This is Gareth Newman. Good evening.

**Sue:** Hi Gareth, this is Sue.

**Presenter:** Nice to hear your voice again, Sue. What've you got to say?

**Sue:** I think we need to give the lad a chance to, um, show what he can do, you know?

**Presenter:** Well, that's a matter of opinion. Of course, you...

incomplete sentence

## Language change

Fashions in spoken language are always changing. For example, the word 'like' is being used more and more in conversation. It is generally used as a **colloquial** word and is more suitable for informal conversation than for formal speech or writing.

So I was like, 'You're so totally not gonna wear that today'.

'Like' is often used to add emphasis or to fill a pause. For example: 'It was a fair result, like' and 'it was, like, awesome'. It is sometimes used to introduce direct speech (see the speech bubble above).

### ACTIVITY 8

Do you use 'like' in conversation? Do your friends and family? Why do people do this? Interview three or four different people and write down what you find out.

### ACTIVITY 9

**a** Think of two other words that you use but people of a different generation, such as your teachers, parents or grandparents, don't use.

**b** Look up each word in a dictionary and, if this word is listed, note down the different meanings connected with it.

**c** Note which uses are Standard English and which are listed as 'informal', 'colloquial', 'slang' or 'non-standard'.

## Variation in spoken language

Spoken language varies hugely. No two people speak in the same way and people rarely speak exactly the same way twice. But the variation follows recognizable patterns and conventions.

A good speaker changes how he or she uses language depending on the situation. The speaker will be aware of:

- **audience:** who he or she is speaking to/who is listening
- **purpose:** why he or she is speaking/what effect he or she is trying to achieve
- **genre:** what type of talk is it: chat, phone call, radio programme, audition or something else.

### ACTIVITY 10

You can present a different version of yourself by changing the way you speak.

**a** Choose one of the situations listed below:

- an audition for a reality TV show
- a telephone call to your employer, explaining that you are sick
- a video presentation about revision techniques for your school website
- an apology to your best friend for an argument the day before.

**b** Role-play the opening words.

**c** Get feedback from others on how effective your use of language was for the situation.

# 2.6 Studying Language and Society

## LEARNING CHECKLIST

In this chapter you will learn to:

1 Understand how spoken language changes to suit different situations.

2 Judge the effect of your own and others' spoken language.

AO2

## Private talk

The spoken language you will study in this chapter is **private**. Private speech takes place between people who are in the same place, at the same time, and who know each other. People use private spoken language in many situations, including:

- outside lessons – such as during break time
- at a social event
- at home with family.

## Spontaneous talk

Most private talk is **unscripted** and **informal**, but some is not. Sometimes the relationship between the speakers is not close or equal, and the conversation might be more formal. There might be a serious topic to discuss and people may take time to think about what they are going to say beforehand.

### ACTIVITY 1

Record two different conversations. For example, one could be between students at school, the other could be between family members at home.

**a** Play back the conversations and complete a copy of the grid below.

**b** How are the conversations different? How does each one reflect the particular place and situation where it took place?

| Points to consider | Conversation 1 | Conversation 2 |
|---|---|---|
| Do the people speak the same amount? Who speaks most? Who speaks least? | | |
| What kinds of non-verbal features show that people are listening, e.g. grunts, hums and other sounds. | | |
| What kinds of words are used? | | |
| Do the speakers challenge or support each other? | | |

UNIT 2

## Formal and informal language

If we are in a formal situation we are likely to use **formal language**. The grid below shows some differences between formal and informal talk.

| Formal spoken language | | Informal spoken language | |
|---|---|---|---|
| standard grammar | "Wouldn't you say?" | dialect or slang | "dontcha?/innit?" |
| standard vocabulary | "...because it was impressive" | abbreviations or vague phrases | "cos it was pretty cool" |
| full sentences | "I plan to go to university." | unfinished utterances | "I'm going to... you know..." |
| formal terms of address | "Mr Carter" | use of first names, nicknames or no name | "Ronnie/hey mate" |

## Informalization of language

Nowadays, informal spoken language is becoming more wide-spread. Even in some formal situations, such as political speeches, people use **informal language** to appeal to a wider, younger audience. For example, Barack Obama often includes colloquial, informal phrases in his speeches, such as 'I get it' and 'Yes, we can'.

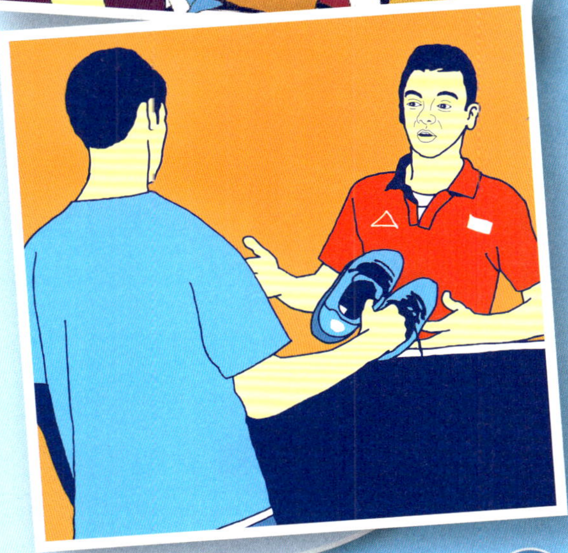

### ACTIVITY 2

With a partner, look at the situations shown on the right. One shows two friends discussing a pair of damaged trainers in a shop. The other shows somebody returning a pair of damaged trainers that he has bought.

**a** Improvise a short scene for each situation using language that you think is suitable.

**b** Show your role-play to another pair, asking them to say which is the formal scene and which is the informal scene.

**c** Ask them whether they think your use of language fits each situation.

## Spoken language in a family situation

A written record of spoken language is known as a **transcript** of speech. Here is a transcript of a conversation between a mother, Anna, her son Jake, and her American daughter-in-law, Kerry. The conversation takes place as they are driving home after a trip to an indoor snow slope.

The use of underlining shows which words are emphasized.

**Jake:** I'm quite proud of myself for not crashing. I thought somebody had come off at the very bottom 'cos when we got there this toboggan [*laughs*] <u>flew</u> past, fractionally missed about three people and crashed into the bottom. Then Kerry pulls up behind me and goes "That's your Mum's" [*laughs*]

**Kerry:** Terrible business [*laughs*]

**Anna:** It wasn't though. I was still on my toboggan.

**Kerry:** Oh, were you <u>still</u>?

**Jake:** 'Cos you did roll a bit.

**Anna:** I know, I was just sort of sitting there really.

**Jake:** Nobody was braking.

**Anna:** The man said "Are you alright?" and I said "Yes".

**Jake:** I think they keep a couple of toboggans on the side 'cos otherwise there's no way for you to get down [*laughs*] It's like "oh well you've just had a nasty fall so we want you to walk down this slippery hill" [*laughs*]

**Anna:** There's no other way to get down. Yeah, so he handed me back my glasses and my hat

**Jake:** ...and a fresh toboggan 'cos yours nearly killed people [*laughs*]

**Kerry:** Oh, terrible business [*laughs*]

**Anna:** Why didn't they say that at the safety talk?

**Jake:** [*laughs*] What, "Don't let go of your toboggan, whatever you do"? [*laughs*]

**Anna:** No, "You can <u>steer</u> to the <u>right</u> but don't just <u>yank</u> the thing or you'll turn it over".

**Kerry:** Kinda common sense?

It's not just words that have meaning in spoken language. The way a person **sounds** also adds meaning: their volume, tone of voice and speed of speaking all create particular impressions.

Silent gaps in the middle of talk are known as **pauses**. Sometimes people pause because they need to take a breath or because they need time to think about what to say next. However, pauses can also signal that the next word is going to be:

- important
- unexpected
- sensitive.

## ACTIVITY 3

Look closely at the transcripts on Page 77 and Page 82.

**a** What are the main differences between them, apart from the topic?

**b** Which one is formal and which one is informal? How can you tell?

**c** In the second transcript, people laugh. What does **when** they laugh tell us about their relationships with one another?

## ACTIVITY 4

Copy and complete the grid below, using the transcript on Page 82 for reference.

**a** Note where you think a pause might be effective for each speaker.

**b** Explain what effect you think each pause may have.

| Speaker | Add extra pause to... | Function of pause |
|---|---|---|
| Jake | 'cos you did (pause) roll a bit | shows that the word 'roll' might be a bit sensitive for Anna, his mum |
| Anna | | |
| Kerry | | |

## Language and social power

In some conversations, one person has more power. This can be seen in **what** they say, in **how much** they say and the **words** that they choose. For example, a powerful boss may use few words but be firm and in control; a good teacher may talk a great deal, using humour and questions.

Who has the power in a conversation is affected by things like age, occupation, gender (whether they are male or female) and situation. People can be powerful in some situations and not in others; for example, a politician may not feel powerful at a toddler's birthday party.

Using powerful spoken language is not just shouting orders. There are other ways of taking control, such as using persuasion, suggestion or encouragement.

### ACTIVITY 5

Imagine passengers facing delays at an airport. Which message from the airline do you think would be most effective and why?

UNIT 2

## Language and gender

The link between language and gender is complicated. Below are some key questions.

- Do males and females have different ways of using language?
- Could this explain problems in relationships?
- Is this the reason why fewer women get top jobs?

### ACTIVITY 6

The grid below lists some common views about language and gender. With a partner, discuss whether you agree or disagree with these opinions. Think of examples to support your ideas.

| Features of spoken language | Females | Males |
|---|---|---|
| how much they talk | more than men | less than women |
| what they talk about | emotions, people | facts, sports and cars |
| vocabulary (words they use) | varied and subtle to show detailed meaning | more general except in areas of speciality, e.g. technical knowledge |
| grammar | exclamations/questions tagged to the end of statements, for example: "You don't want that, do you?" | statements, orders |
| taboo language | avoid rude words | swear a lot |

## Giving instructions

In a classroom many instructions are given out to students. You might expect the spoken language of teachers to be made up of lots of orders such as, 'Do this.... /Listen to this... /Read the passage...'. These verbs are known as **imperatives**.

However, most teachers use a variety of spoken strategies. These strategies include replacing imperatives with:

- questions
- statements
- exclamations.

### ACTIVITY 7

**a** Match each speech bubble below to the 'real' order (imperative) that the teacher is giving on the right.

1 Have you finished?

2 You don't need to shout.

3 What a helpful comment!

**Imperative sentences**

**a.** Don't shout.
**b.** Don't be so awkward.
**c.** Hurry up.

**b** What has the imperative been replaced with in each case? A question, a statement or an exclamation?

**c** Why do you think a teacher might use these strategies rather than just using imperatives?

## ACTIVITY 8

The same strategies can be used in the workplace, at home or with friends. Copy and complete the grid to show how language can be used in this way.

| Situation | Indirect spoken language | Direct meaning |
|---|---|---|
| You come home late one evening with some friends. | 'You're making a lot of noise.' | 'Be quiet.' |
| You want to get a lift from your parents to a friend's house. | 'I really need to do this work at Sarah's.' | |
| You want to borrow some money from your friend. | | 'Give me a fiver.' |

## Language and occupation

We adapt our spoken language according to what we are doing and who we are with. Some jobs have their own **specialized vocabulary** or **jargon** which can be confusing to outsiders.

Some jobs not only have their own jargon, but staff are trained to speak in a certain way, particularly when talking to customers. In sales jobs, for example, employees may be trained to use persuasive techniques to influence customers.

## ACTIVITY 9

Choose a topic that interests you; for example, sport, fashion or music.

**a** Make a list of the specialized jargon that 'outsiders' may not be familiar with.

**b** Exchange your list with a partner and talk about the terms you recognize and those you are unfamiliar with.

**c** Think of two advantages and two disadvantages of using jargon in speech.

# PREPARING FOR UNIT 2

## SECTION B: SPOKEN LANGUAGE

### How will my work be marked?

You will be marked on Assessment Objective 2, which tests the skills below.

- **Understand variations in spoken language, explaining why language changes in relation to contexts.**

  This simply means understanding how spoken language changes to suit different situations.

  We all have different types of speech, depending on who we are speaking to and what our purpose is. The language you use at home when talking to your family will be different from the language you use at school when speaking to your teachers.

  People use different language for different **purposes**; for example, to persuade others, to give instructions or to entertain each other. People also use different language in different **situations**; like attending a job interview or chatting to a friend on the phone.

- **Evaluate the impact of spoken language choices in your own and others' use.**

  This simply means judging the effect of your own and others' spoken language.

  We are all influenced by the way other people speak. This might make us want to copy their style or go completely the opposite way. For example, how would you want to sound if you were trying to encourage people to give money to charity? What language choices would you make if you wanted to break up with your boyfriend or girlfriend?

The way you speak might be influenced by language that you have heard in the past: someone you saw on a news programme; even lines from a character in your favourite soap.

A good way to prepare for this assessment is to try to think carefully about people you hear talking on the radio or that you see and hear talking on TV. As well as people in the media, listen to people speaking socially and in more formal situations.

## How will the task be presented?

Your teacher will give you advice about what you need to cover in this Controlled Assessment. You may take notes into your assessment and you are also allowed to take in unmarked transcripts of speech for reference.

# Unit 3

## Information and Ideas

## HOW TO APPROACH UNIT 3

### What is covered in this unit?

This unit tests your reading and writing skills. The reading texts will be **non-fiction** and the writing will be **informative** writing.

### How will I be assessed?

You will sit an exam, with unseen texts and writing tasks. **Unseen** means that you will not have studied the texts beforehand in class. The exam will count for 40% of your English Language GCSE.

You will have **two hours** to complete the exam. There is no word limit for your writing but the **quality** is always more important than the **quantity** of your work.

### What will be in the exam?

The exam is divided into two sections, each worth **40 marks**.

- In **Section A** you will be given two texts to read. One will be non-fiction and the other a media piece. They will be linked in some way.
- In **Section B** you will have a choice of two tasks. Each task will ask you to complete a particular form of writing (for example, a letter or talk) and to write for a particular audience.

## SECTION A: NON-FICTION AND MEDIA

In this section you will be marked according to Assessment Objective 3, which tests the skills listed below.

- Read and understand texts, selecting material appropriate to purpose, gathering evidence from different sources and making comparisons and cross references as appropriate.
- Develop and sustain understanding of writers' ideas and points of view.
- Explain and explore how writers use language, structure and presentational features to engage and influence the reader.

# 3.1 Non-Fiction: How Meaning is Constructed

## LEARNING CHECKLIST

AO3

In this chapter, you will learn to:

1. Understand texts, choosing parts that are related to certain ideas and comparing them where necessary.
2. Explain how writers use language, style and form to interest the reader and to make the reader think a certain way.

## Reading non-fiction texts

This chapter is about **non-fiction texts**, such as advice leaflets in a doctor's surgery or articles in a holiday brochure. Writers deliberately craft their texts to have an effect on you, the reader, for example, to persuade you to do something, to entertain you or to give you information. Read the following extract from a leaflet advertising an adventure park.

alliteration makes the name memorable

Bored with the sofa? Ready for new challenges? Looking for a day out with friends?

**THE OUTRAGEOUS OUTDOORS CENTRE**

### WHAT WE OFFER

Outrageous Outdoors is the best place to find adventure and exhilaration. Our centre includes: a first-rate zipwire, high speed go-carting, abseiling, climbing, caving, quad biking, assault courses, arcades and water sports.

list shows large variety of activities to appeal to different people

99% of visitors who visited last year rated their day at the centre as 'fantastic'.

statistic emphasizes that visitors enjoy themselves

'I've never had a better day with my mates. There is so much choice.' *Gurpreet, 15*

opinion shows that it is fun and sociable

'The races, competitions and team games mean that everyone gets involved.' *Mohammed, 16*

### TRAINED INSTRUCTORS

Our fully trained and experienced staff will provide you with all the guidance you need to make the most of our activities.

09867 43576959

www.outrageousoutdoors1000.co.uk

## Persuasive techniques

When writing a persuasive text, authors often include certain features or techniques. These features can be remembered using the mnemonic: **A FOREST**.

| Terms | Definitions |
|---|---|
| Alliteration | words that begin with the same sound (e.g. fantastic features) |
| Facts | points that can be proven |
| Opinions | what someone thinks or believes |
| Repetition and rhetorical questions | repeated words or phrases, and questions that make you think but do not require an answer |
| Emotion | words and ideas that stir strong feeling in the reader |
| Statistics | figures to support ideas or arguments (e.g. 92% of people believe exercise is good for you) |
| Three | the power of three or more things in a list. Lists can show options, give examples or emphasize reasons |

### ACTIVITY 1

Look at the leaflet on Page 92. Find examples of as many of the **A FOREST** features as you can. Suggest how each feature might influence the reader.

### FUNCTIONAL SKILLS TASK

FUNCTIONAL SKILLS

Look in a local newspaper for adverts for activities to do or hobbies to try out. Read each advertisement carefully and find three techniques that persuade you to try out the activity.

## Structure, sentences and words

The structure of a text is important. A good, clear text has a specific opening, middle and end, and each paragraph focuses on a specific topic or theme.

Read the email below. The writer is trying to persuade a friend to go to a gig.

**RE: GIG ON FRIDAY NIGHT**

**From:** jo117@musicworld.com
**To:** alexsummers@musicworld.com

---

Hi,

What are you up to at the moment? It's been a while since I've seen you. We should get together to catch up.

Have you ever been to the exhibition centre in town? It's massive. They have all sorts of events there; it's an ideal place for music. In fact, this Friday there's something on. The exhibition people have invited our favourite band. They will also have loads of other music: new bands and bands looking to be signed. Before and after the gig, we can get our CDs signed. Haven't you always wanted to see them up close?

If you're worried about what your parents will say, don't be. It's an event for under 18s. There will be security and no random people without tickets will be allowed in. I can get my dad to give us a lift and pick us up.

And don't worry about the cost! It's only a fiver each and Dad giving us a lift will save us money. There will be CDs and t-shirts on sale but we don't have to buy any of that. You can come round to mine and eat before we go. Then we'll only have to worry about drinks. It'll be so hot in there with all of those people (the atmosphere will be wild!); we'll only need water.

Let me know as soon as you can so that I can buy the tickets. Say hello to everyone for me. Looking forward to seeing you,

One of your best mates!

The email on Page 94 has a clear structure and the writer has thought carefully about sentences and word choices. Do you think the writing is effective? If this friend had emailed you, would you have agreed to go to the gig?

## ACTIVITY 2

**a** Think of a title for each of the paragraphs in the email. The first one could be 'greeting'.

**b** Name two things the writer thinks may put her friend off going to the gig.

**c** Do you think she deals with those well? Explain your answer by referring to the text.

## FUNCTIONAL SKILLS TASK

FUNCTIONAL SKILLS

Find leaflets for different events in your local area – perhaps from the library or tourist information centre.

- What persuasive techniques have been used?
- Look at the information provided in each leaflet – is it all necessary? Is anything important missing?
- Is it appealing to look at or would it be easily overlooked among other leaflets?
- Of the leaflets you have collected, which one do you think is the most effective? Why?

## Formality and style

At home and with friends, most people chat informally. At other times, for example, when attending a job interview, we have to use more formal language. It is the same when you write.

Read the letter of application below.

16th July 2011

Miss Laura Gwent,
16 Butterfield Street,
Chauchester
CS36 SDL

Mr Greggs,
VClothes,
10 Winterfield Road,
Chauchester
CS45 7XL

I am writing to apply for the position of shop assistant at VClothes as advertised in the Local Herald on 10th July.

I am currently studying eight GCSEs at Crossworth School, Chauchester. I am a reliable and trustworthy student who is looking forward to gaining more work experience. I attended two weeks of work experience at Bravo Superstores last month showing that I have the skills required to be a shop assistant. My employer particularly commented on my hardworking approach and punctuality.

At school, it is predicted that I will pass all of my GCSEs. I am studying catering which means that I have learnt to be polite when working with customers during our catering events.

My interests show that I have a sense of humour and can meet a challenge. I am interested in TV comedies and climbing.

I am in the last year of school and hope that a weekend job at your store will help me in my ambition to work in retail.

Finally, please do not hesitate to contact me for further details or references.

Yours sincerely,

Laura Gwent

## ACTIVITY 3

**a** Which words or phrases help to create the formal tone of the letter? Look up any words that you do not understand.

**b** Look at the structure of the letter. Give each paragraph a title.

**c** The main purpose of this letter is to give the reader information. How well do you think the writer does this? Explain your answer by referring to the text.

## ACTIVITY 4

**a** Choose one of the job advertisements below and write a letter of application. (You can invent the addresses and names.) Use ideas from the letter on Page 96 to help you. Remember to use **formal words**.

**b** Peer assessment: Swap your letter with a partner.

- Check that your partner's letter includes formal words. If any informal words are used, suggest formal alternatives.
- Decide whether you would offer your partner an interview on the basis of the letter. If not, explain why and suggest ways to improve it.

**Café seeks confident person** to take orders at the counter. Must be able to greet people enthusiastically and politely! Hours negotiable. **£8 per hour.**

**Dog walker wanted.** Once a day, five times a week, 20 minutes per day. Must love dogs. Must be reliable and trustworthy. Two references essential.

## FUNCTIONAL SKILLS TASK

FUNCTIONAL SKILLS

- In groups of three or four, collect several adverts for weekend jobs in your local area. You could look online or in your local newspaper.
- You are going to write a draft letter of application for one of the jobs advertised. In your group, choose the advert that is the most interesting.
- Each member of the group should write their own letter of application. Include information that is relevant and use a suitable structure and style.
- Read the letters as a group. Decide which is the strongest and why.

## Promotional texts

**Some writing has more than one purpose. Imagine a computer games company wants to develop a new game. It is doing a survey on its website, giving readers promotional texts for two possible games. It is asking readers which game they would be most likely to buy. The promotional texts below give information as well as trying to persuade the reader that the game is worth buying.**

### Destiny Detectives

You will take the role of one of five detectives as you travel through the most famous cities in the world. Explore each living, breathing city on foot or in one of a range of authentic vehicles, speaking to residents and uncovering clues. Each suspect will have their own story to tell – but don't be fooled by appearances!

Every decision you make, every word you speak will have consequences on how the game pans out. You will need to think carefully, act quickly and make the most of your environment to be successful.

The cities have been re-created in amazing high definition, with a music score from Hollywood's top composers. This is more than just a game, this is an experience you will never forget!

### Real Racing

Real Racing: the next best thing to being behind the wheel. You don't even need to earn the best car. We'll throw it in at the beginning. Start with a fantasy car. Then trash it in an obstacle-filled track. Now, start all over again…

With so many cars to choose from, wreck, and choose again, you won't get bored with this racer. Customize your car from the suspension up, or select one of over 50 pre-configured rides. Then tear up the track in over 20 breathtaking locations.

Take to the road in cities including London, New York, Paris and Tokyo. Have your friends join in the action with team-based or competitive online matches. Your game, your rules.

More restless and rapid than the rest: Real Racing.

## ACTIVITY 5

Often the writers of promotional texts will use a number of different writing techniques and devices.

Copy and complete the grid below.

| | Examples | |
|---|---|---|
| **Technique** | **Destiny Detectives** | **Real Racing** |
| alliteration | | |
| common, informal phrases | | |
| rhetorical questions | | |
| exaggeration | This is more than just a game | |
| jargon | | |
| imperatives (verbs that give an order) | | Take to the road |
| punctuation for emphasis | | |
| lists | | |
| repetition | | |

**a** Find examples of the techniques listed above in the promotional texts on Page 98.

**b** Choose three techniques from those you have found. What effect do you think the writer wants to create with them? Refer to the text in your answer.
For example:

Alliteration is used to make the title of the game memorable and emphasizes the word 'real'. 'Real Racing' makes the reader imagine that the game will be as good as racing a real car.

## Reviews

When reading a text, it is important to think about the **way** it is written and **how effective** it is rather than just focusing on what it is about. Read the user reviews, below, from a film website.

*Silent Screams? More like Loud Laughs.* This film is not at all as scary as the trailers suggested: the actors couldn't act; the set shook every time someone walked past; and the over-used close-ups added nothing but humour. Low-budget movies can be fantastic. However, this was 120 minutes with absolutely no build up of tension, suspense or drama.

Are you looking for a horror movie? Avoid *Silent Screams*. Looking for a comedy? *Silent Screams* is just right.

FilmBuff26 ★

technical language

comments on who might enjoy the film

*Better Now than Later*: Action and sci-fi films are my thing. This was an average film. The story was interesting because it was about a boy who was able to drive at the age of 13. His parents owned a race track. Then we find out that his car is actually a robot that is radio-controlled by alien intelligence. The aliens are green and live in cars not houses. The aliens think that humans should be used like slaves. Then the action starts. He is thrown into a war where he has to crash into lots of other cars without dying. He has a friend who helps him. In the end, we find out that the boy is actually a robot.

actionhero007 ★★★

comments on the plot

Romantic comedies are great. I watched *Love in the Heart of New York* last night. I really enjoyed it. The actors were interesting. You should go to see this film. It is one and a half hours long. You will enjoy it. It is really good. It is romantic and funny.

Romcom3 ★★★★

personal opinion

comment on the actors

## ACTIVITY 6

In pairs, discuss which film review is the most effective. Explain why, with close reference to the text.

## ACTIVITY 7

Write a review for a website or newspaper about a film you have watched. First, think about the audience and then use a suitable tone and vocabulary to keep them interested.

Your review could include:

- your overall opinion of the film
- comments on the acting and actors
- brief details about the plot or how the film begins
- the special effects
- suggestions as to who would enjoy the film
- a summary of your opinion at the end.

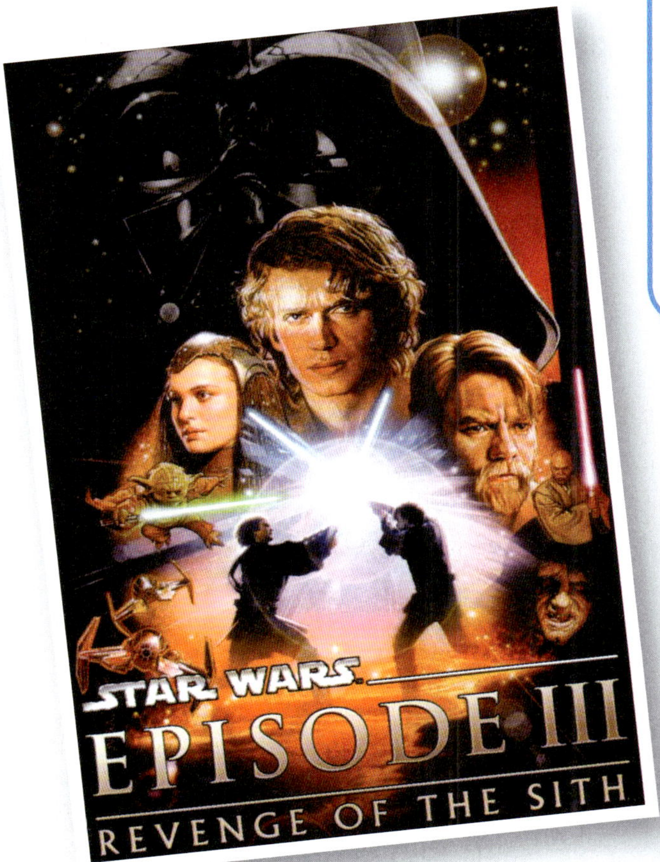

## FUNCTIONAL SKILLS TASK

Look up a film, music or computer game website and read some of the online reviews. Take three or four reviews and compare the quality of each one. Look at:

- the language techniques used by each writer and how effective they are
- how well the writer keeps to the task of reviewing (rather than just retelling the story)
- how effectively the writer conveys his or her opinion.

FUNCTIONAL SKILLS

# 3.2 Evaluating How Texts are Interpreted

**LEARNING CHECKLIST**

In this chapter, you will learn to:

1 Understand texts, choosing parts that are related to certain ideas and comparing them where necessary.

2 Interpret writers' ideas and points of view (viewpoints).

3 Explain how writers use language, style and form to interest the reader and make them think a certain way.

AO3

## Understanding viewpoints

People often have different viewpoints on the same situation. Some people's views may be **subjective** (shaped by personal feelings). For example, people who live close to a youth club might object to it because they dislike the noise.

Other people's views may be **objective** (not linked to personal feelings). For example, they may be in favour of a youth club because they believe young people should have a safe place to meet friends.

The grid on the right contains some key terms related to viewpoints.

| Key terms | Definition |
|---|---|
| perspective | the way that someone looks at or thinks about something |
| bias | something that influences your opinion and can lead to your opinion becoming one-sided |
| objective | not influenced by personal feelings |
| subjective | influenced by personal feelings |
| balanced argument | an argument that looks at all opinions and ideas before coming to a conclusion |

**ACTIVITY 1**

Which key terms would you link with the following statements? (You can choose more than one term per answer.)

**a** 'The children make too much noise. The park should close!'

**b** '88% of the people surveyed wanted to keep the park open.'

**c** 'I can see why parents want the park to stay open. However, it would be more useful to more people to have a supermarket there.'

## Letters to an MP

When presenting an argument to someone specific, a writer may choose to use a formal letter to add importance to his or her point of view.

**ACTIVITY 2**

Read the two etters below. Who do you think will suffer most from the closure of the ɔark? Use the information in the letters to back up your opinion.

Dear Mr Graves MP,

I am very concerned that a park in your constituency is about to be closed. The park is just 200 metres from my home. I go to the park every day. However, it is not just for my sake that I write this letter. Many other retired people use the park as they see it as a safe area to get some fresh air and exercise. Many pensioners have little money. The park is free and a great break from sitting in the house. This is good for our mental well-being, physical health and overall comfort.

Furthermore, young children, parents and teenagers also use the park. At least 150 people visit every day. A lot of your constituents will be upset if this open area is barred from them.

Finally, have you visited the park? It is the most beautiful space. There is a play area for toddlers and climbing frames for older children. Many teenagers play football there. It is welcome relief from the grey of the city.

Yours sincerely,

Ben Amos

clear opening statement

personal information

introduces objective view

pattern of three to emphasize benefits

statistic backs up argument

rhetorical question challenges the reader

emotive image

Dear Mr Graves MP,

I am disappointed to hear that the council plans to close Greenfield Park. I am a local person who uses the park twice daily. I walk my dog and enjoy the fresh air. Where will I take my dog if the park is closed? In fact, where will all of the young children and teenagers go? Please act now to save our park!

I will encourage other people to write to the council to show their displeasure. I enclose a picture of my dog, Rex. How could you deny this lovely dog his favourite activity?

Yours sincerely,

Gurpal Singh

subjective viewpoint

rhetorical questions convey urgent concern

direct plea is emotive

outlines future action

## A different viewpoint

The extract below is from a supermarket website. The supermarket chain is interested in buying land to build a new supermarket.

**BUDGET**
*More for Less*

ABOUT US | SPECIAL BUYS | CAREERS | INFO | STORE LOCATOR

### We're getting bigger and better!

Since opening our first store ten years ago, BUDGET has successfully established itself as one of the leading retailers in Europe.

We put our customers first, offering them amazing choice and quality of products at prices that everyone can afford.

Our success means that we are following an ambitious expansion programme, constantly seeking new employees, suppliers and premises.

### Make us an offer!

Our investment programme means that we are looking for new sites, located in towns with a population of more than 8,000.

We are interested in:

- buying land that can be developed
- leasing existing buildings in town centres.

Our promise to you...

- an efficient, business approach
- competitive pricing
- a generous commission package.

Get in touch now and together we can invest in a bright, affordable future for our customers.

### ACTIVITY 3

**a** What is the main purpose of this webpage?

**b** How does the writer use presentation to make his or her message effective? (Think about the layout, picture, headings, use of bullets, slogan and logo.)

## A campaign leaflet

Some people write campaign leaflets to make their views public and to persuade others to take action with them. Read the 'Shoppers Unite!' campaign leaflet on the right.

### ACTIVITY 4

People might respond to this leaflet in different ways.

**a** Explain how this leaflet may persuade some people to join Shoppers Unite.

**b** Explain how this leaflet may make other people more determined to keep the park.

### FUNCTIONAL SKILLS TASK

In pairs or small groups, write your own campaign leaflet about an issue you feel strongly about. You need to:

- get your message across quickly and strongly
- use repetition for effect
- be persuasive, using strong arguments
- make it clear what you want people to do, for example, sign a petition, donate money or take part in a march.

# Reports

To write a report, information is collected, people are interviewed and surveys are carried out. This information is then put together under different headings. Good reports are **objective** and will give a conclusion and make recommendations at the end.

## Report on the Health of Students at Heartswell School

### Aim of this report

This report aims to identify ways in which students at Heartswell School can be supported to improve their health.

### School meals

Students are offered meals with a low salt, sugar and fat content. Every meal includes vegetables. However, only 60% of students eat school dinners. 8% eat nothing. We have no data about what 32% of our students eat at lunchtime.

### Home meals

Students completed a food diary about what they eat at home after school. 76% of students ate sweets or chocolate every day. 56% of students ate crisps or chips every day. In the survey, 38% of students stated that they ate five portions of fruit and vegetables every day.

### Physical Education department

All year groups have to do physical education for two hours per week. This should continue. However, on average, 11% of students do not take part in PE owing to injury or illness.

### Out of school exercise

In the survey, it was shown that 37% of students took part in team games such as football at least once a week. Another 23% of students take part in another form of exercise such as swimming or running.

### Recommendations

- Design and complete another survey to find out how to encourage more students to eat school dinners.
- Offer free fruit at break times.
- Explore the alternatives to eating chips, crisps, sweets and other unhealthy foods as part of PSHE lessons.
- Have regular free tasting sessions for the school dinners and suggest ideas for alternative healthy snacks to eat at home.
- Start a Saturday sports club where students can play football and hockey.

## ACTIVITY 5

**a** Is the report on Page 106 written in an **objective** or **subjective** style? Give reasons for your answer.

**b** Why do you think that the report uses facts and statistics? Choose two examples and explain what effect these have on the reader.

## ACTIVITY 6

Copy and complete the grid below to show possible reactions to the report's recommendations. Try to include a range of different opinions.

| | Parent | Student | PE Teacher | School Meals Manager | Head Teacher |
|---|---|---|---|---|---|
| Positive reactions to the report | It would be good to encourage students to eat more fruit. I like the sound of the free tastings. | | | | |
| Negative reactions to the report | Packed lunches are cheaper than school dinners and I know they will eat them! | | | It will cost money to give free tastings. | |

## Presenting a counter-argument

Below is a letter to the Head Teacher at Heartswell School about the report on Page 106.

Dear Mr Edwards,

We have met and discussed the report on the health of students. While we are happy that you have chosen to investigate this topic and plan to take action to improve health, we do have some concerns.

We are unhappy about the recommendations in the survey about home meals and packed lunches. After discussion, we have decided that students should not be encouraged to eat school dinners. We believe that students should be able to eat as they choose. This is a free country and secondary school students are old enough to make their own choices.

Furthermore, we are concerned that you are insisting on two hours of Physical Education per week. In our brief survey, 70% of students stated that they disliked PE. Students are able to find their own exercise and sports outside of school.

Thank you for considering our opinion.

### ACTIVITY 7

**a** Who do you think this letter is from? Explain your answer using evidence from the text.

**b** How does the writer of the letter present a counter-argument (the opposite view) to the recommendations given in the report on Page 106?

**c** Do you agree with this reaction to the report? Explain your answer, by referring to the text.

## Interpreting the writer's viewpoint

In your exam, you will need to show the examiner that:

- you have a clear understanding of the writer's viewpoint
- you can back up your ideas with evidence from the text.

The activities in this chapter focus on understanding different viewpoints. The checklist on the right will help you to do this effectively.

Viewpoint checklist

- What is the writer's point of view?
- What evidence can you find in the text to back this up?
- What tone does the writer use? (E.g. Is it humorous, serious or light-hearted?)

# Trouble sleeping?

**MAKE YOUR BEDROOM A PLACE OF REST**

Do you spend night after night lying awake, unable to drop off? Did you know that you are much more likely to have difficulty sleeping if your bedroom is filled with distractions?

How many electrical devices do you have in your bedroom? Do you have a TV, computer and a mobile? Anything else? Your bedroom should be a place of rest. It should not be a place where you stay awake until the early hours watching TV or playing computer games. Unlike your TV, you need time to switch off. This means time to do nothing before you go to sleep.

Have you ever had a night's sleep interrupted by a mobile phone? Turn it off! Once your sleep is broken, it can be difficult to nod off again.

So – before you resort to counting sheep, make sure everything is switched off!

**OTHER THINGS YOU CAN DO**

- **Don't eat just before going to bed.**
- **Go to bed at the same time each night.**
- **Avoid drinking tea and coffee after 6pm.**

### ACTIVITY 8

With a partner, discuss the text above and decide what you think the writer's point of view is. Write a paragraph explaining this point of view, using the checklist to help you.

# PREPARING FOR UNIT 3

## SECTION A: NON-FICTION AND MEDIA

### What will the questions be like?

This is the reading task. You will have **one hour** in the exam to complete the reading and write your responses. You will need to answer **two** questions.

- **Question 1** will focus on **reading for information**. This means that you will be asked to select relevant parts of the text and put these into your own words.
- **Question 2** will focus on **reading for interpretation**. This means that you will be asked to look at **how** things are said, so you need to focus on the presentation, style and layout, and how this can be interpreted by the reader.

### How should I divide my time in the exam?

You should expect to spend up to 25% of the time reading and thinking before you start to write. Candidates who start writing immediately are less likely to gain good marks for their responses.

# HOW TO APPROACH UNIT 3

## SECTION B: WRITING INFORMATION AND IDEAS

### What will I be assessed on?

In this section you will be marked according to Assessment Objective 4, which tests these skills:

- Write clearly, effectively and imaginatively.
- Use forms and choose vocabulary which is correct for the task and purpose and engages the reader.
- Organize information and ideas into sentences, paragraphs and whole texts, using language and structure to make sure that they fit together well.
- Use a range of sentence structures to make your writing clear and effective.
- Use accurate punctuation and spelling.

3.3

# Choosing Content, Style and Language

**LEARNING CHECKLIST**

AO4

In this chapter you will learn to:

1 Write clearly, with imagination, using a suitable form and words to interest the reader.

2 Write in sentences and paragraphs, using a clear structure and order, and a variety of language features and techniques.

3 Use different sentence structures to create different effects, with correct punctuation and spelling.

## Using suitable form and words

Writing is all about balance. When you are given a writing task you need to decide:

- how formal it should be
- what style, layout and tone to use
- what sort of words and sentences are appropriate.

The scale below shows the choices that you have to make.

1 ⟷ 10

| Informal | Formal |
|---|---|
| Light-hearted | Serious |
| Emotive | Impersonal |

UNIT 3

**ACTIVITY 1**

Look at the different types of texts below:

a teenage magazine article on fashion

a job application letter

a text message to wish a friend good luck

a review of a film

Use the scale above to help you answer the following questions.

**a** Which text is likely to be the most formal?

**b** Which text do you think would be the most opinionated?

## Planning a piece of writing

Before completing a piece of writing you need to consider several things:

- its purpose
- your audience
- the layout
- the style.

The mnemonic 'PALS', shown in the grid below, may help you to plan your work and to check it afterwards.

For example, if you wanted write a complaint your purpose would be to **explain** the problem to the organization responsible and also to **persuade** them to do something about it. You would use a formal letter layout with clear paragraphs and your tone would be serious and probably quite annoyed.

| Term | Explanation |
|---|---|
| **P**urpose | Why are you writing?<br>Are you writing to entertain, persuade, report, explain, review or something else? |
| **A**udience | Who are you writing for?<br>A friend, a boss, a teacher, an MP or someone else? |
| **L**ayout | Should you write your text in paragraphs? Does it need subheadings or bullet points? Does it need a letter layout? |
| **S**tyle | What tone should your text be written in: lively, light-hearted, serious, thoughtful, angry? Should you use the first person (I), third person (he, she, it) or second person (you)? |

### ACTIVITY 2

**a** Plan an article for your local newspaper about a film festival at your school. At the festival, visitors, parents and students were invited to watch short films by students and vote for the best one. Use the PALS mnemonic, in the grid, to help you plan.

**b** Write the article in full.

## Different types of writing

Different types of writing generally use certain features or 'ingredients'. When you are given a writing task, you need to understand what type of writing it is and the sort of features that are usually included.

In the panels below are examples of some of the main features and techniques used for different types of writing. Some types of writing mix more than one style, for example, a travel guide may give factual information but also include description and advice. It all depends on the **purpose** of your text and its **audience**.

### ACTIVITY 3

Match the following texts to their type (or types) below:

**a** a recipe

**b** a webpage comparing prices of mobile phones

**c** a magazine article about whether school students should be allowed to work from home on the Internet

**d** a piece of writing giving the writer's opinion of a film.

**Report**

- headings and subheadings
- formal language
- facts, figures and statistics
- clear and simple layout
- recommendations and/or conclusions at the end

**Review**

- gives reasons why the product or experience is good or bad
- gives a conclusion
- often uses technical language or jargon
- gives an opinion, often subjective
- sometimes uses comparison
- gives a conclusion

**Writing to argue**

- balanced and objective
- gives arguments for and/or against a topic
- comes to a conclusion after considering the facts
- uses connectives, e.g. however, furthermore, moreover, similarly, etc.
- often uses comparison

**Writing to give instructions**

- clear and factual style
- uses imperative verbs, e.g. get, put, cut, take etc.
- often uses subheadings
- impersonal tone (avoids using he, she, we or I)
- uses connectives, e.g. first, next, finally, before etc.

## Structure: beginnings and endings

The beginning of a text is important as it sets the tone and style of your writing. The ending of a text is important because it leaves the reader with a final impression of what you want to say.

Below are some example beginnings and endings:

1

2

The best gadgets are friendly, fun and easy to use.

3

I hope that you feel better soon.
We all miss you,
The Rangers Family

4

I know that you will support our campaign to help our most endangered animals.

Yours sincerely, Emily Hanover

### ACTIVITY 4

**a** With a partner, discuss what types of text the extracts above might come from.

**b** Write a beginning and ending for each of the following tasks:
- a magazine article looking at the effects of binge drinking
- an email to a company asking them to donate products for a charity auction.

**c** Compare your beginning and ending for each text with a partner. Which are the best sentences? Why?

### FUNCTIONAL SKILLS TASK

FUNCTIONAL SKILLS

A friend is writing a letter to the council about noisy neighbours. Look at the way he has started and ended the letter. What advice would you give him about letter writing?

> Mr Patel,
>
> I am furious! When are you going to do something? You lot are useless!
> [...]
> Never mind sorting out the rubbish, drains and roads! Kick out my neighbours!
>
> Yours angrily,
>
> A Friend

## Language techniques: tone

To create a successful piece of writing you need to think carefully about your **tone**. The words on the right describe different tones:

friendly

angry

tense

sympathetic

lively

enthusiastic

humorous

business-like

frustrated

light-hearted

### ACTIVITY 5

**a** Identify the tone (or tones) used in each of the three extracts below on the right.

**b** Write the first paragraph for an article on smoking for a teenage magazine.

- First, write it in a serious, formal tone for people worried about their health.
- Next, write it in a lively way to engage (interest) young people and encourage them to think about the dangers of smoking.

**1** Walk to town? She must be mad. It's miles away! It would take us all night to get there!

**2** The ball was midair when Trouth nudged it to the right, out of Carlton's reach.

**3** We can all do our bit to help save the planet: walking rather than driving; switching off lights; turning down the heating. None of this requires too much effort does it?

### FUNCTIONAL SKILLS TASK

Write a letter of complaint to a cinema (about the noise, price or length of the queues). Ask a partner to comment on how effective your use of **tone** is in your writing (i.e. is it likely to achieve the result you want?).

FUNCTIONAL SKILLS

## Choosing the style of your writing

Many texts, such as magazine articles, mix together a range of language and structural features. Before you write your response in the exam, you need to decide what **style** you are going to use. This should depend on your topic and your target audience.

Below are some extracts from magazine articles, showing headlines and first lines.

1

HEALTH:
Mobile Phones
Scientists fear that mobiles could damage your health.

2

Top Ten Days in the UK
Looking for something to do this weekend?

3

Pet Show Stars
A beagle bursts into rhythmic barks to the theme tune of *Animal Zoo*.

4

LITTER LOUTS
Smith investigates how you feel about the idea of fines for people who drop litter.

### ACTIVITY 6

**a** With a partner, discuss the possible **purpose** of each article above.

**b** What **tone** of language would you expect the writer to use in each article?

**c** What other language features would you expect to find in each?

## Style and audience

Read the recipes below. The annotations highlight features that affect the style of each text.

### Super Sleek Sundae

Buy the best ice cream, fresh fruit and cream you can find. Raspberries, strawberries and blueberries work well.

- Cut the fruit into chunks ready to be blitzed in the liquidizer. If you don't have a liquidizer, you could chop the fruit into small pieces, then mash it with a spoon.
- Take a sneaky taste of the sauce and if necessary add a tablespoon of sugar. Taste again. Add more sugar if you like.
- Splash the fruit into a saucepan and heat gently.
- Whip up the cream until it is thick enough to pick up a scoop with your finger.
- Use your best glasses to present the sundae in all its glory. Pour in a little warm fruit sauce, then a scoop of ice cream, a scoop of cream and repeat.
- Finish with a little more sauce. Delicious!

choice of vocabulary

use of pronouns

level of detail

### Fruit Sundae

Ingredients

200g soft fruit (strawberries, raspberries or blueberries)

two tablespoons unrefined cane sugar

high-quality vanilla ice cream

300ml double cream

1 First, roughly halve or chop the fruit.
2 Liquidize the fruit and add sugar to taste.
3 Gently simmer the fruit to heat it.
4 Whip the cream until it is firm.
5 Finally, layer the ice cream, fruit and cream in a tall glass. Serve.

choice of headings

layout of information

sentence structure

### ACTIVITY 7

What sort of audience do you think each recipe above is aimed at? Think about the tone, style and vocabulary.

### FUNCTIONAL SKILLS TASK

Choose a recipe from a book or the Internet. Change the tone and style to make it more suitable for a specific audience, for example, children or people who don't enjoy cooking.

FUNCTIONAL SKILLS

UNIT 3

## Practise planning and writing

You could use the diagram below to help you plan a writing task.

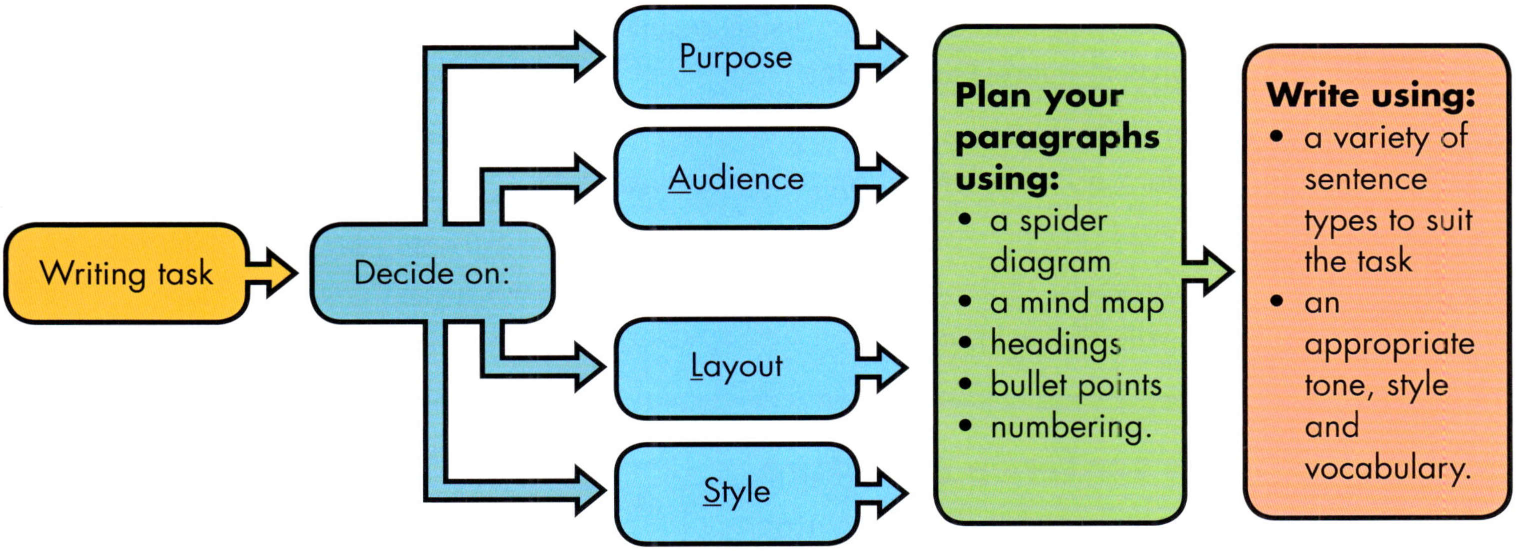


### ACTIVITY 8

Plan a magazine article about the dangers of sunbathing. Copy and complete the grid below in as much detail as possible.

| | **Magazine article on the dangers of sunbathing** |
|---|---|
| Purpose | |
| Audience | |
| Layout | |
| Style | |

# Adapting Form to a Range of Styles and Genres

## LEARNING CHECKLIST

AO4

In this chapter you will learn to:

1. Write clearly, with imagination, using a suitable form and words to interest the reader.
2. Write in sentences and paragraphs, using a clear structure and order and a variety of language features and techniques.
3. Use a variety of sentence structures to create different effects, with correct punctuation and spelling.

## Variety in sentence structure

To create an interesting piece of writing, you need to make your sentences varied, using different sentence structures.

Using a range of punctuation can also add variety to your sentence types; for example, using question marks and exclamation marks.

### ACTIVITY 1

Write your own short paragraph on the subject of homework. Use a mix of sentence structures and types to make your writing varied and interesting for the reader.

an exclamation to show how strongly the writer feels

a rhetorical question to make the reader think

Exams! Who needs them? I can live without them. However, qualifications are important if you want to do further education or if you want to find a job. But there always seems to be more interesting things to do than schoolwork, even if it's just tidying my room!

a simple sentence with just one idea in it

a list of ideas in a complex sentence

## Connectives

Connectives act like glue – they fix ideas together in sentences and connect sentences together in paragraphs. Without them a text can seem like a random selection of ideas without a logical flow between them.

Connectives can do different jobs. They can show time or allow the writer to give a reason for something. They can also help to organize information.

although

if

while

then

but

since

eventually

before

therefore

or

unless

however

as

after

### ACTIVITY 2

**a** Choose three connectives from those above and write three example sentences for each one. Remember that connectives can go at the start or in the middle of sentences. For example:

The striker scored a magnificent goal <u>before</u> being sent off the pitch.

**b** Then, for each example, explain to a partner what job the connective is doing.

## Sorting out paragraphs

Your writing will have more logic and style if you think about how ideas are grouped together into paragraphs.

Here are some of the main topics that can be the focus of paragraphs, or the reason to begin another one:

- introduction or conclusion
- place
- time
- direct speech (when someone speaks)
- change of topic.

**ACTIVITY 3**

Look at the extract from a website below and decide the purpose of each paragraph. Use the list on the left to help you.

**DERWENTVALLEYMILLS**

**Info** | Photos

In December 2001, the Derwent Valley Mills in Derbyshire became a World Heritage Site. This international designation confirms the importance of the area as the birthplace of the factory system.

*international designation: a category which is recognised all over the world*

Here, in the 18th century, water power was successfully harnessed for textile production. This brought hundreds of workers together in one place and changed employment in the valley from agriculture to industry in the first 'modern' factories.

*harnessed: used*

The Derwent Valley Site stretches for 15 miles from Matlock Bath to Derby. It contains a fascinating series of historic mills and workers' cottages and is ideally placed for a holiday base. Why not pay a visit?

Regular guided tours are given by local volunteers who possess a wealth of knowledge on the area's history. Click here for details.

## Letters and reports

The form and structure of informal letters, emails and text messages can be quite straightforward. Formal letters and reports are often more complicated. Use this chart to remind yourself of some key features:

| Formal letter | Formal report |
|---|---|
| Include your address and the date on the right-hand side. | Use a title which states the subject briefly. Who is it for? |
| Put the name and address of the person you are writing to on the left-hand side. | First paragraph outlines topic. |
| 'Dear Mr Smith,' ends with 'Yours sincerely,' and a signature. 'Dear Sir/Madam,' ends with 'Yours faithfully,' and a signature. | Later paragraphs explore points fully. |
| State the subject clearly in the first paragraph, then continue. | Final paragraph gives recommendations. |

### FUNCTIONAL SKILLS TASK

In pairs, discuss the format needed for the following tasks, and then write one of them:

- a report on the benefits of owning a pet
- a letter to the editor of your local paper about the dangerous state of a children's playground in the park.

## Webpages and leaflets

We get lots of information from websites and leaflets – anything from world news to ticket prices for music gigs. Webpages and leaflets use visual clues to guide their readers through the content. Look at some examples of these features below:

- captions
- headings and subheadings
- video clips
- lists/tables
- inset boxes with key facts
- bullet points
- hyperlinks
- question and answer sections
- Photos, maps and diagrams
- different fonts, use of bold and italics, underlining

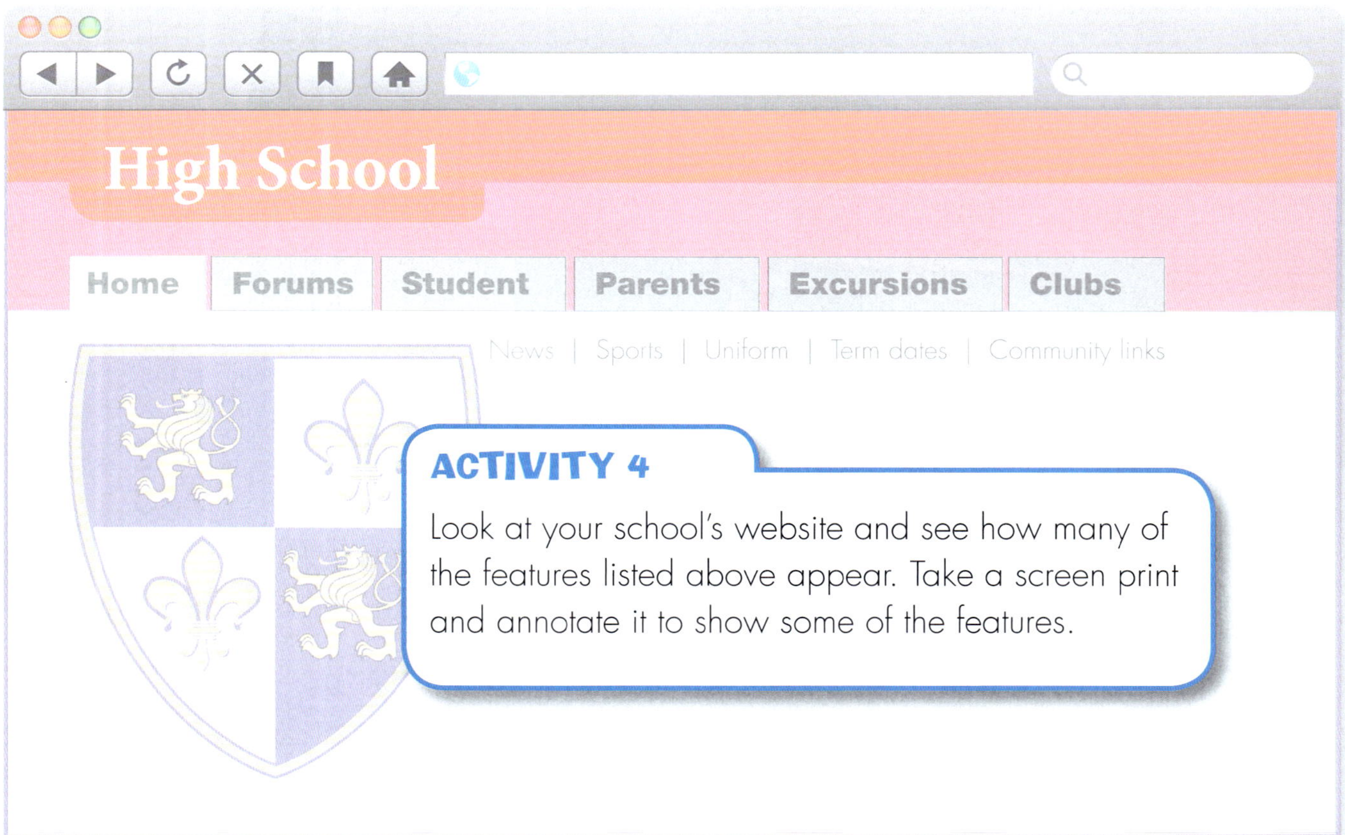


**ACTIVITY 4**

Look at your school's website and see how many of the features listed above appear. Take a screen print and annotate it to show some of the features.

## Newspaper reports

Newspaper reports should always aim to explain **what** happened, **where** and **when** it happened, **who** was involved, and if possible, **how** and **why** it happened.

They usually have a **standfirst** paragraph at the beginning, which summarizes the key points of the story.

thepaper

# Ice Scream!

eye-catching headline

**With their raucous calls and greedy appetite, gulls are a distinctive feature of the British seaside, but relations with humans are becoming strained during the summer months.**

standfirst introduces topic

when

who

where

Holidaymakers in Skegness have complained of being 'mugged' by hungry seagulls stealing chips, sandwiches and ice cream.

what – the main issue

One visitor, 8 year-old Chelsey Barnes, said, 'I was really scared. It was like a monster attacking me.'

quotation

emotive language

Seafront caterers feel the tourists themselves are often to blame. Jamie Wigs, owner of the 'Seafood Delights' stall says 'Tourists often throw bits of food to the gulls, tempting them to come closer, but then get alarmed when the gulls start to eye up the food in their hands.'

alternative viewpoint

### ACTIVITY 5

Write a newspaper report about whether or not dogs should be allowed on beaches. Remember to use the style and features of a newspaper report.

**a** Plan your report using the grid below to help you.

| Feature | Example |
|---|---|
| what? (main topic/issue) | |
| where? | |
| when? | |
| who? | |
| standfirst | |
| alternative viewpoint(s) | |
| headline | |
| quotations | |
| emotive language | |

**b** Write a draft of your report.

**c** Swap with a partner and check one another's work.

**d** Write up your final draft.

## Consolidating your writing skills

Before you tackle any writing activity, there are questions you need to ask yourself. Remember to use 'PALS' to help you to plan:

**Purpose:** why are you writing?

**Audience:** who are you writing for?

**Layout:** how should the text be structured and presented?

**Style:** what tone should it be written in? What vocabulary would be appropriate?

UNIT 3

### ACTIVITY 6

Write an article for your school newspaper complaining about coverage of music on television. Use the PALS mnemonic to help you plan your article.

### FUNCTIONAL SKILLS TASK

FUNCTIONAL SKILLS

You work for an environmental charity and you are in charge of a campaign to promote a more 'green' way of living. Create a webpage to inform the general public about ways they can make their lifestyles more eco-friendly. Think about which **style**, **tone**, **language** and **layout** features will be most effective.

# PREPARING FOR UNIT 3

## SECTION B: WRITING INFORMATION AND IDEAS

### What will the task require me to do?

You will need to write **one** piece of extended writing from a choice of two. You have **one hour** to complete this task and it is worth **40 marks**.

The task will tell you everything that you need to know, so read it carefully.

- **Background:** the task will give a context for the writing, e.g. who you are writing as and why you are writing.
- **Main task:** this explains what you need to write, in what form, e.g. a letter or a newspaper article.
- **Prompts:** given as bullet points, suggesting what to cover and even some possible starting sentences.

### How can I do my best in the exam?

To get the best results in the exam, you need to practise. Try using the approach below to ensure you make the most of your time.

Make sure you understand the **audience** you are writing for and the **form** you have to use.

→ Plan your work, starting with an engaging **opening**, followed by **linked paragraphs** and a final **conclusion**.

→ At the end, make sure that you go back and **check** your work for mistakes.

OXFORD
UNIVERSITY PRESS

Oxford University Press is a department of the University of Oxford. It furthers the University's objective of excellence in research, scholarship, and education by publishing worldwide in

Oxford New York

Auckland Cape Town Dar es Salaam Hong Kong Karachi Kuala Lumpur Madrid Melbourne Mexico City Nairobi New Delhi Shanghai Taipei Toronto

With offices in

Argentina Austria Brazil Chile Czech Republic France Greece Guatemala Hungary Italy Japan South Korea Poland Portugal Singapore Switzerland Thailand Turkey Ukraine Vietnam

Oxford is a registered trade mark of Oxford University Press in the UK and in certain other countries

© Oxford University Press 2011

Authors: Chris Barcock, Liz Hanton, Mel Peeling, Alison Ross, Alison Smith, Christine Shaw Smith

The moral rights of the authors have been asserted.

Database right Oxford University Press (maker)

First published 2011

All rights reserved. No part of this publication may be reproduced, stored in a retrieval system, or transmitted in any form or by any means, without the prior permission in writing of Oxford University Press, or as expressly permitted by law, or under terms agreed with the appropriate reprographics rights organization. Enquiries concerning reproduction outside the scope of the above should be sent to the Rights Department, Oxford University Press, at the address above.

You must not circulate this book in any other binding or cover and you must impose this same condition on any acquirer

Third party website addresses referred to in this publication are provided by Oxford University Press in good faith and for information only and Oxford University Press disclaims any responsibility for the material contained therein.

British Library Cataloguing in Publication Data
Data available

ISBN: 978-0-19-832949-7

10 9 8 7 6 5 4 3 2 1

Printed in Spain by Cayfosa-Impresia Ibérica.

**Acknowledgements**
The publisher and authors would like to thank the following for their permission to reproduce photographs and other copyright material:
**p11**: Diana Taliun/Shutterstock; **p12t**: Moviworld/MK2/Miramax/The Kobal Collection; **p12–13**: Bettmann/Corbis; **p14**: Photodisc/OUP; **p16**: Mary Evans Picture Library; **p17**: Everett Collection/Rex Features; **p18–19**: Radomir Rezny/Dreamstime; **p19m**: Sean Gladwell/Shutterstock; wessley/Shutterstock; **p20l**: Imperial War Museum; **p20r**: Mary Evans Picture Library/Photolibrary; **p21**: Mary Evans Picture Library/Photolibrary; **p22**: Bildarchiv Preussischer Kulturbesitz; **p24t**: Monkey Business Images/Shutterstock; **p24m**: R. Gino Santa Maria/Shutterstock; **p24b**: Gelpi/Shutterstock; **p25**: Timo Kohlbacher/Shutterstock; **p26**: Dan Bannister/Shutterstock; **p27**: Susannah Ireland/Rex Features; **p29t**: Kieran Doherty/Reuters; **p29b**: Kieran Doherty/Reuters; **p31**: Mehmet Dilsiz/Shutterstock; **p35**: Eleanor Bentall/Corbis; **p37**: kristian sekulic/Shutterstock; **p43**: Bruce Shippee/Fotolia; **p44t**: Yellowj/Shutterstock; **p44b**: Celso Pupo/Shutterstock; **p46**: Ken Fitzpatrick; **p49t**: CandyBoxPhoto/Shutterstock; **p49b**: HANA/Shutterstock; **p56**: Somos/OUP; **p57**: Deshacam/Dreamstime; **p58**: Rune Johansen/Photolibrary; **p59**: Simon Winnall/Photolibrary; **p63**: Mark J. Terrill/AP Photo; **p64**: Rex Features; **p65**: Back Page Images/Rex Features; **p66**: Comstock/OUP; **p67**: Tony Dejak/AP Photo; **p68t**: Rui Vieira/PA Archive/Press Association Images; **p68b**: Adrian Sherratt/Rex Features; **p69**: Ken McKay/Rex Features; **p70**: Jeffrey Blackler/Alamy; **p71**: Ross D. Franklin/AP Photo; **p72**: rangizzz/Shutterstock; **p75**: Monkey Business Images/Shutterstock; **p77**: Andre Maritz/Shutterstock; **p79l**: Emmanuel Faure/Stone/Getty Images; **p79r**: Objectif MC/Shutterstock; **p82**: Global Warming Images/Alamy; **p87**: StockLite/Shutterstock; **p92**: Oez/Shutterstock; **p94**: DW Photos/Shutterstock; **p95t**: Roel Loopers/Photolibrary; **p95b**: Becky Stares/Shutterstock; **p97**: Christopher Hall/Fotolia; **p99**: Monkey Business Images/Shutterstock; **p100**: Joe Belanger/Shutterstock; **p101l**: The Ronald Grant Archive; **p101r**: The Ronald Grant Archive; **p102**: Magone/Shutterstock; **p104**: OUP; **p105**: Paul Clarke/Shutterstock; **p106t**: Brett Mulcahy/Shutterstock; **p106m**: Surkov Vladimir/Shutterstock; **p106b**: Photodisc/OUP; **p108t**: Dennis Macdonald/Photolibrary; **p108b**: Chris King/OUP; **p116**: Yobidaba/Shutterstock; **p118**: Monkey Business Images/Shutterstock; **p119**: Ivanova Inga/Shutterstock; **p122**: Derwent Valley Mills Partnership; **p123**: Péter Gudella/Shutterstock; **p124**: scusi0-9/Shutterstock; **p125**: Le Do/Shutterstock; **p126**: GLUE STOCK/Shutterstock.

Illustrations by Ben Swift, Flora Douville, Oxford Designers & Illustrators, Rheannon Cummins, Theresa Tibbetts, Tom Genower.

The publisher and authors are grateful for permission to reprint the following copyright material:
**Simon Armitage**: 'About his Person' from *Kid* (Faber, 1992), copyright © Simon Armitage 1992, reprinted by permission of Faber & Faber Ltd.
**Bill Bryson:** extracts from *Notes from a Small Island* (Black Swan, 1996), reprinted by permission of The Random House Group Ltd.
**Carol Ann Duffy:** 'Stealing' from *Selling Manhattan* (Anvil, 1987), reprinted by permission of Anvil Press Poetry.
**Stephen Fry:** extract from *Stephen Fry in America* (HarperCollins, 2008), copyright © Stephen Fry 2008, reprinted by permission of HarperCollins Publishers Ltd.
**Athol Fugard:** extracts from *Tsotsi* (Canongate, 2009), originally published by Ad Donker, South Africa 1980 and in Australia by The Text Publishing Co, reprinted by permission of the publishers, Canongate Books, 14 High Street, Edinburgh EH1 1TE, Text Publishing Co, and DALRO Pty Ltd, South Africa on behalf of Ad Donker.
**Nikki Garnett:** extract on Morecambe from www.citycoastcountryside.co.uk, reprinted by permission of the author and Apparatus Marketing.
**Mark Haddon:** opening extract from *The Curious Incident of the Dog in the Night-Time* (David Fickling/Jonathan Cape, 2003), reprinted by permission of The Random House Group Ltd.
**Annabel Kenzie:** extracts from 'The Beautiful Game' in *Smart English: Progress in Afs* (Smart Learning), reprinted by permission of the author.
**John Steinbeck:** extracts from *Of Mice and Men* (Penguin, 2006), copyright © John Steinbeck 1937, 1965, reprinted by permission of Penguin Books Ltd.
**Jonathan Tulloch:** extracts from *The Season Ticket* (Jonathan Cape, 2000), reprinted by permission of The Random House Group Ltd.
**John Wyndham:** opening extract from *The Chrysalids* (Michael Joseph 1955, Penguin Books 1958, 1979, 2000), reprinted by permission of David Higham Associates.
**Benjamin Zephaniah:** 'Three Black Males' and lines from 'Chant of a Homesick Nigga' from *Too Black, Too Strong* (Bloodaxe, 2003), reprinted by permission of Bloodaxe Books.

Although we have made every effort to trace and contact all copyright holders before publication this has not been possible in all cases. If notified, the publisher will rectify any errors or omissions at the earliest opportunity.